HALLOWEEN RECIPE BOOK

THIS BOOK BELONGS TO

_____

_____

_____

TABLE OF CONTENTS

Halloween Layer Cake 4

Reese's Bats 6

Spooky Ghost Cookies 7

Candy Corn Cobs 9

Rosemary-Pumpkin Seed Brittle 10

Mummy Pumpkin Hand Pies 11

Marshmallow Ghost Brownies 12

Spiced Pumpkin-Molasses Cake 14

Pumpkin-Spiced Buns with Spiderweb Glaze 15

Spider Cookie Truffles 17

Coffin Sandwich Cookies 18

Liquid Web Cocktails 20

Smokey Pumpkin Deviled Eggs 21

Hats and Bats Chocolate-Peanut Butter Tarts 22

Spooky Forest Pudding Cups 24

Towering Haunted House Cake 25

Black-Bottom Brownies 28

"Poison" Candy Apples 30

Spiced Chocolate Bat Cookies 31

Peanut Butter Acorns 33

Meringue Ghost Tartlets 34

Chocolate Pumpkin Witch Cupcakes 35

Cereal Bar Hay Bales 37

Almond Shortbread Owls 38

Brown Butter-Hazelnut Blondies 40

Cookies Magnifying Glass Cookies 41

Devil's Food Cupcakes 43

Footprints Malted Sheet Cake 44

Basic Sugar Cookie Dough 45

Apple-Cardamom Cakes with Apple Cider Icing	46
Cookie Cutter Ginger Crisps	48
Pumpkin Mousse	49
Maple Cupcakes	51
Upside-Down Pear Tartlets	52
Sweet Popcorn Balls	53
Marbled Chocolate Bark	54
Turtle Corn	55
Peanut butter monsters	56
Chocolate Peanut Butter Bars	57
Bloody Truffles	58
Jack Skellington Cheesecakes	60
MUMMY COOKIES RECIPE	62
Halloween Popcorn Balls	63
Double Chocolate Cookie Bark	65
Meringue Ghost Tarts	66
Candied Clementines	68
Cookie Bat Cupcakes	69
Red Velvet Cookies	70
Moss Cookies	71
Halloween Snack Mix	72
Spiderweb Cake	73
Halloween Cake Pops	76
Black Cat Cookies	78
Chocolate Skeleton Cookie Cupcakes	79
Frankenstein Cake	79
Witch Cupcakes	83
Spiderweb Cupcakes	84
Fossil Cookies	85
Dark Chocolate Candy Cookies	86
Pecan Pie Bars	87
Bat Sandwich Cookies	88

Graveyard Cupcakes 89

Black and Red Crinkle Cookies 90

Mummy Cupcakes..91

Chocolate and Pumpkin Ice Cream Sandwiches 91

Chocolate Skeleton Cookies 92

Stuffed Dark Chocolate Whoopie Pies..93

Chocolate Pumpkin Cake 95

Halloween Layer Cake

YIELDS: 16 SERVINGS

PREP TIME: 0 HOURS 30 MINS

TOTAL TIME: 2 HOURS 0 MINS

INGREDIENTS

FOR THE CAKE

- Nonstick cooking spray for pans
- 1 box Devil's Food cake mix, plus additional ingredients as directed on the box
- 1 box vanilla cake mix, plus other ingredients as directed on the box

PURPOSES OF FROSTING

- 2 c. (4 sticks) softened butter
- 7 c. divided powdered sugar
- 1 and a half cups whole milk
- 2 tbsp. unsweetened vanilla extract

- 2 teaspoon pumpkin pie spice
- Food coloring in orange

FOR THE GANACHE AND ASSEMBLY
- 1 1/2 cup chocolate chips, semisweet
- 3/4 cup unsweetened condensed milk
- Peeps with Ghosts
- Milano biscuits
- Crushed Oreos
- Confectionery corn
- Sugared pumpkins
- Sprinkles
- Chocolate eyeballs

DIRECTIONS

1. heat oven 350 degrees and lightly spray four 9-inch cake pans with cooking spray. Prepare both chocolate and vanilla cake batters in two large mixing bowls using a hand mixer.
2. Divide batter evenly between prepared pans, two chocolate, and two vanilla, and bake for 30 min, or until a toothpick inserted in the center comes out clean. Cool completely on a wire rack.
3. In another large mixing bowl, to make the frosting, beat together the butter and half of the powdered sugar until smooth using a hand mixer. Add the milk, vanilla extract, pumpkin spice, and remaining powdered sugar and beat until light and fluffy. Stir in food coloring until the frosting is a vibrant orange reminiscent of a jack-o-lantern.

4. Heat heavy cream in a small saucepan over low heat until it bubbles to make the ganache. Combine chocolate chips and hot, heavy cream in a medium, heatproof bowl. Allow 2 minutes before whisking until smooth.
5. Assemble the cake: Level the cake layers using a big serrated knife. Spread a dab of frosting and top with the first vanilla cake layer on a cake plate or serving platter.
6. Spread 1 c. frosting on top of the cake and spread into a uniform layer. On top of that, layer the first chocolate cake and coat it with another cup of frosting. Repeat with the remaining vanilla and chocolate layers. Frost the outside of the cake with the remainder of the icing.
7. Drizzle ganache down the cake's sides, then pour the remaining ganache on top and smooth with an offset spatula.
8. Assemble the cake: Create a graveyard scene by sticking ghost peeps on skewers and arranging them on the cake as graves. Surround the graves with Oreo "soil," sprinkles, candy corn and pumpkins, and candy eyeballs.

Reese's Bats

YIELDS: 10

PREP TIME: 0 HOURS 15 MINS

TOTAL TIME: 0 HOURS 15 MINS

INGREDIENTS

- 10 miniature Reese's cups
- five Oreos

- Twenty candy eyes
- 1 tbsp. unsalted peanut butter

DIRECTIONS

1. Halve all Oreo cookies and gently scrape out the cream. Each half should be cut in half to make the wings.
2. Apply a little dab of peanut butter to one end of each Oreo using a toothpick or a small spoon. To create wings, press onto Reese's cup.
3. Next, dab a small amount of peanut butter onto the backs of two candy eyes and lay them on top of the wing edges. Serve.

Spooky Ghost Cookies

YIELDS: 24
PREP TIME: 0 HOURS 10 MINS
TOTAL TIME: 2 HOURS 0 MINS

INGREDIENTS

FOR THE COOKIE DOUGH

- 3 c. all-purpose flour, plus additional flour for the surface
- 1 tsp. bicarbonate of soda
- 1 teaspoon kosher salt
- 1 cup (2 sticks) softened butter
- 1 cup sugar, granulated
- 1 extra-large egg
- 1 tablespoon milk
- 1 tsp. unsweetened pure vanilla extract

APPROPRIATE FOR ROYAL ICING

- 3 tablespoons powdered sugar
- 1/4 cup corn syrup, light
- 1/4 cup milk, plus additional milk for thinning
- 1/4 tsp almond extract
- Food coloring in black

DIRECTIONS

1. Whisk flour, baking powder, and salt in a mixing bowl.
2. Cream butter and sugar in a large mixing dish. Beat the egg, milk, and vanilla extract until incorporated, then add the flour mixture in a slow, steady stream until combined. Form a disk and refrigerate for 1 hour.
3. Preheat the oven to 350oF and line two large baking pans with parchment paper. Roll out dough until it is 1/8" thick on a lightly floured work surface. Cut out cookies with a ghost cookie cutter. Reroll scraps and continue cutting out cookies. Freeze the mixture for ten minutes on the prepared baking sheets.
4. Bake for 8 to 10 minutes, or until the sides are lightly brown. Cool thoroughly on a wire cooling rack.
5. In the meantime, prepare the icing: Combine powdered sugar, corn syrup, milk, and almond extract in a medium bowl.
6. Place about 1/4 of the icing in a small bowl and tint it black with black food coloring.
7. Using approximately half of the white frosting, pipe edges around cookies using a piping bag fitted with a small round tip.
8. Add 1 teaspoon of milk to the remaining white icing until it runs efficiently on cookies but is not watery. Fill the centers of the cookies

with frosting using another piping bag fitted with a small round tip. Utilize a toothpick to burst any air bubbles and distribute icing to fill any gaps. Allow cookies to dry for 15 minutes or until the icing is set.

9. Insert a tiny round tip piping bag with black icing and pipe eyes and mouths onto cookies.

Candy Corn Cobs

YIELDS:12

PREP TIME:0 HOURS 5 MINS

TOTAL TIME:3 HOURS 30 MINS

INGREDIENTS

- 1/2 cup (1 stick) softened butter
- 1/2 cup sugar, granulated
- 1 tsp. unsweetened pure vanilla extract
- 1 cup blanched almond flour
- 1 tablespoon kosher salt
- 2 (20-oz.) candy corn bags

DIRECTIONS

1. In a mixing bowl, beat butter and sugar with a hand mixer until smooth, then add vanilla. Mix in the almond flour and salt. The dough should be divided into four equal pieces. Form each part into a log using plastic wrap. Refrigerate for 2 hours or until solid.
2. Once the cookie dough has been thoroughly chilled, put candy corn into the dough in rows. Refrigerate for 1 hour before serving.

Rosemary-Pumpkin Seed Brittle

YIELDS: 12 servings

TOTAL TIME: 0 hours 55 mins

INGREDIENTS

- 1 and a half cup granulated sugar
- 1/2 cup (1 stick) sliced unsalted butter
- 1 and a third cup golden syrup
- 1/2 tsp. bicarbonate of soda
- 2 1/2 cup pepitas, roasted and salted
- 1 tbsp. fresh rosemary, chopped
- 1 and 1/4 teaspoon freshly ground black pepper
- Sea salt with large flake

DIRECTIONS

1. preheat oven to 350°F. Parchment paper a rimmed baking sheet. In a saucepan, combine sugar, butter, and golden syrup. Over medium-high heat, bring to a boil. Cook for 10–15 minutes, without stirring, until light brown and a candy thermometer reads 300°F.

2. Take the pan off the heat and carefully stir in the baking soda (mixture will bubble up). Stir in pepitas, rosemary, and pepper quickly. Scrape brittle immediately onto the prepared baking sheet and spread evenly into a thin, even layer. Season with salt. Allow 35 to 45 minutes to cool completely. Dismantle.

Mummy Pumpkin Hand Pies

YIELDS: 12 servings

TOTAL TIME: 3 hours 45 mins

INGREDIENTS

- 2 1/2 cups flour, spooned and smoothed, plus additional flour for the work surface
- 3 tbsp. Plus 2 tsp. divided granulated sugar, with more for sprinkling
- 1 tsp. kosher salt plus a sprinkle, divided
- 1 cup cold unsalted butter, sliced
- 3 oz. room temperature cream cheese
- 1/2 cup pure canned pumpkin
- 1 large egg plus 1 yolk of an egg, divided
- 1 and 1/2 teaspoon pumpkin pie spice
- 1 and a half teaspoon pure vanilla extract
- Twenty-four delicious candy eyeballs

DIRECTIONS

1. pulse flour, 2 tablespoons sugar, and 1 teaspoon salt four to five times in a food processor. Add butter and pulse 12 to 15 times, or until the mixture resembles a coarse meal with a few pea-size bits left. Add 5 tsp ice-cold water, 1 tsp at a time, pulsing just until the dough comes together (add up to an additional tsp of water, if needed). Divide dough into two equal portions; knead together and wrap each piece in plastic wrap. Flatten and press dough into loose rectangles using plastic wrap. Refrigerate for 2 hours or until hard.

2. In a separate bowl, beat cream cheese until smooth 1 minute. With electric mixer on medium speed, beat pumpkin, egg yolk, pie spice, vanilla, a pinch of salt, and remaining 3 tablespoons sugar until smooth, about 2 to 3 minutes.

3. preheat oven to 350°F. Line two baking pans with parchment paper. Roll dough to a 1/4-inch thickness, working with one piece of dough at a time on a lightly floured work surface. Divide the dough into six three-by-four-inch rectangles. Transfer to baking sheets that have been prepared. Rep with the remainder of the dough. Spread a rounded tablespoonful of pumpkin mixture on top of each rectangle, leaving a 1/2-inch border around the borders.

4. Reroll bits of dough by kneading them together. Cut into 1/4 inch broad by 5 inch long strips. Hand pies should be topped with multiple overlapping slices to resemble a mummy. With your fingertips, seal the edges and trim excess.

5. In a bowl, whisk together the egg and 1 tablespoon of water. Strips should be lightly brushed with egg wash and sprinkled with sugar. Allow 20 minutes for cooling.

6. Preheat the oven to 400 °F. Bake for 20–25 minutes until browned. Allow 20 minutes to cool. Mummies should have sugary eyes.

Marshmallow Ghost Brownies

YIELDS:12 - 16 servings

TOTAL TIME:2 hours 50 mins

INGREDIENTS

For the Brownies:

- Nonstick cooking spray

- 1 cup plus 2 tablespoons all-purpose flour, leveled with a spoon
- 1 and a half teaspoon pumpkin pie spice
- 1/4 tsp. bicarbonate of soda
- 1 teaspoon kosher salt
- 1 cup chocolate chips, semisweet
- 9 tbsp (1 stick plus 1 tablespoon) butter unsalted
- 1/4 cup chocolate powder, unsweetened
- 1 and a half cups sugar
- 3/4 cup pureed pumpkin
- 3 sizable eggs
- 1 tsp. unsweetened pure vanilla extract

Dedicated to the Marshmallow Ghosts:

- 1 1/4 teaspoon gelatin, unflavored (part of 1 envelope)
- 1/2 cup sugar, granulated
- Black piping icing from the store

DIRECTIONS

Construct the Brownies:

1. heat oven 350 degrees F. Line a 9-by-13-inch baking dish with parchment paper, leaving a 2-inch overhang on both sides. Grease the parchment paper.
2. Whisk together flour, pie spice, baking powder, and salt in a bowl. In a saucepan over medium heat, melt chocolate chips, butter, and cocoa, occasionally stirring, until smooth, about 2 to 3 minutes. Whisk together sugar, pumpkin puree, eggs, and vanilla extract in a second dish. Stir the

butter mixture into the sugar mixture until combined. Stir in flour mixture until combined. Transfer to the pan that has been prepared.

3. Bake 20 to 22 minutes, or until a toothpick inserted in the center comes out with a few moist crumbs attached. Remove and cool completely on a wire rack. Run a knife along the pan's two short sides and use parchment to pull the pan. Transfer brownies to a serving plate, parchment paper removed.

Create the Marshmallow Ghosts as follows:

1. To soften gelatin, sprinkle 1/4 cup of cold water over it in a bowl.
2. In a saucepan, combine sugar and 1/4 cup of water. Cook, constantly stirring, until sugar is melted, 1 to 2 minutes. When the water reaches a boil, stop stirring and use a damp pastry brush to wipe along the edges of the pan to remove any undissolved sugar and prevent crystals from forming. To make candy, boil for 4–6 minutes or till 238°F.
3. Combine sugar and gelatin in a bowl. Whisk for 3 minutes on a medium speed with an electric mixer. Increase speed to high and whisk for 8 to 10 minutes, or until soft peaks form. Transfer marshmallows to a large zip-top bag with a small hole cut in one corner.
4. Pipe ghost shapes onto brownies immediately. Allow 1 hour for drying. Black icing eyes and mouths should be piped. Brownies can be stored for 1 day in an airtight container.

Spiced Pumpkin-Molasses Cake

YIELDS:10 servings

PREP TIME:0 hours 0 mins

TOTAL TIME: 2 hours 25 mins

INGREDIENTS

- Nonstick cooking spray
- 3 c. cake flour, leveled with a spoon
- 1 tbsp. spice blend for pumpkin pie
- 1 tsp. bicarbonate of soda
- 1 tsp. baking powder
- kosher salt, 1 tsp.
- 1 cup molasses
- 1 cup pure pumpkin puree
- 1 and 3/4 cup buttermilk
- 1/2 cup vegetable oil
- a single huge egg
- Sucrose for confectioners

DIRECTIONS

1. heat oven 350 degrees F. Grease a 10-inch circular cake pan lightly. In a large mixing basin, whisk together flour, pie spice, baking soda, baking powder, and salt; create a well in the center of the mixture. Whisk together the molasses, pumpkin, buttermilk, oil, and egg in a separate basin. Mix wet and dry components well. Transfer to the pan that has been prepared.
2. In the center, insert a wooden pick and bake for 50–55 minutes. After 10 minutes, transfer the cake onto the wire rack to complete cooking.
3. Dust with confectioners' sugar before serving, using a decorative parchment pepper stencil.

Pumpkin-Spiced Buns with Spiderweb Glaze

YIELDS: 12

TOTAL TIME: 2 hours 40 mins

INGREDIENTS

- 1/2 cup warm whole milk (100 to 110 degrees F)
- 2 (1/4-ounce) active dry yeast packets
- 2/3 cup split packed light brown sugar
- 3/4 cups flour, spooned and smoothed, plus additional flour for the work surface
- 1 and 1/2 teaspoon kosher salt
- 14 tbsp. (1 3/4 sticks) unsalted butter, at room temperature, split
- 1 cup pure canned pumpkin, split
- 2 big room-temperature eggs
- 2 tablespoons confectioners' sugar
- 6 oz. room temperature cream cheese
- 1 tsp. unsweetened pure vanilla essence

DIRECTIONS

1. Grease a basin lightly. In a second bowl, combine milk and yeast. Allow standing for 4 to 5 minutes until frothy (if the yeast does not foam, discard and start again). Combine 1/3 cup brown sugar and 1 cup flour in a medium bowl. Beat on low speed with an electric mixer fitted with a dough hook until incorporated, about 1 to 2 minutes. Add salt, 1 teaspoon pumpkin pie spice, and 6 tablespoons butter and beat for 1 minute or until smooth. Add 3/4 cup pumpkin and beat until smooth, 1 to 2 min. Beat in eggs one at a time, until mixed. Beat in 3 3/4 cups flour in a slow, steady stream for 1 minute, or until incorporated.

2. For a loose dough that pulls away from the sides of the bowl, increase mixer speed to medium for 1 minute (dough will still stick to the bottom of the

bowl). Continue beating for 3 to 5 minutes, or until dough is smooth and elastic. Turn dough in the prepared bowl to coat. Cover with a clean dish towel and allow to double in size in a warm location (80°F to 85°F), 45 minutes to 1 hour, or refrigerate overnight.

3. Combine the remaining 8 tablespoons of butter and 1/4 cup pumpkin in a dish. Combine the 1/3 cup brown sugar and 1 teaspoon pumpkin pie spice in a second bowl.

4. Pinch the dough together and turn it onto a lightly floured work surface. Roll up the dough into a 12-by-16-inch rectangle. Cover the dough with butter mixture, leaving a 1/2-inch border around the edges. Sprinkle with brown sugar mixture, gently pressing to ensure adhesion. Trim the dough on both ends.

Parchment paper a big rimmed baking sheet. Serrated knife 12 identical slices of dough Arrange on a prepared baking sheet. Cover with a clean dish towel for 30-40 minutes to rise.

6. Preheat oven to 350°F. Bake for 20–25 minutes, or until golden. Allow 10 minutes for cooling on a wire rack.

7. In a medium mixing basin, whisk together confectioners' sugar, cream cheese, and vanilla extract until smooth. Transfer the mixture to a zip-top bag. Make a 1/4-inch hole in one of the bag's corners. Pipe glaze in a spiderweb pattern on top of buns. Serve immediately.

Spider Cookie Truffles

YIELDS:36

TOTAL TIME:2 hours 30 mins

INGREDIENTS

- 36 sandwich cookies with chocolate
- 1 (8-ounce) container room temperature cream cheese, cut into pieces
- 2 (12-ounce) packages of melted semisweet chocolate chips
- edible Candy eyeballs
- String licorice in black, cut into 2-inch pieces

DIRECTIONS

1. Line a baking sheet with wax paper. Pulse cookies until fine crumbs form in a food processor, about 30 seconds. Add cream cheese and pulse 15–20 times until mixed. Make 1 1/4-inch ball with the mixture and set it on a prepared baking sheet. Freeze for 1 hour or until firm.

2. Dip cookies in chocolate and place them back on the baking sheet. Add edible candy eyeballs and black thread licorice for decoration. Refrigerate for 1 hour or until set.

Coffin Sandwich Cookies

YIELDS: 34 servings

TOTAL TIME: 3 hours 45 mins

INGREDIENTS

For the Cookies:

- 1 tbsp. cornstarch
- 2 tbsp. chocolate powder, unsweetened
- 3 kosher salt, 3/4 tsp.
- 1 cup (2 sticks) softened unsalted butter
- 1 cup light brown sugar, packed

- 1 tbsp. molasses
- 2 extra-large eggs
- 5 cups plain flour, spooned and leveled

White Chocolate Bones:

- 1/2 cup candy melts white chocolate

Prepare the Buttercream Filling as follows:

- 1/2 cup (1 stick) softened unsalted butter
- 1 1/2 cup confectioners' sugar, sifted
- Pure vanilla extract, 1/4 tsp.
- 1 kosher salt pinch
- Food coloring in the color red
- Food coloring in orange

To be used with the Royal Icing

- 1 and a half cups confectioners' sugar
- 2 tbsp. powdered meringue
- Food coloring in black

DIRECTIONS

Prepare cookies:

1. Preheat oven to 375 °F. Preheat oven to 350°F. Line four baking pans with parchment paper. In a bowl, whisk together cornstarch, cocoa, and salt.

2. With an electric mixer on speed, beat butter and sugar until light and fluffy, about 2 to 4 minutes. Add molasses and beat for 1 minute, or until completely combined. Add eggs one at a time, scraping down the sides and bottom of the bowl between additions. Reduce mixer speed to a low setting and add

cornstarch mixture. Add flour and beat just until combined. Wrap each part in plastic wrap and flatten. Refrigerate for at least one hour and up to two days.

3. On a floured work surface, roll dough to a thickness of 3/8 inch. With a 3-inch coffin cookie cutter, cut coffin shapes; move to prepared baking sheets. Bake 8 to 9 minutes, or until cookies are firm around the edges but still somewhat soft in the center.

Prepare white chocolate bones as follows:

Melt candy melts as directed. Snip a hole in one corner of a zip-top bag and transfer it. Melted candies should be poured into the bone mold. Chill for 20 to 30 min, or until firm. Remove from molds with a tap.

Prepare the filling:

Beat butter with an electric mixer until smooth and creamy on a medium speed, about 1 to 2 minutes. Add confectioners' sugar in 1/2 cup increments, mixing well after each addition and regularly scraping down the bowl's sides. Incorporate vanilla and salt. To create a deep orange color, combine red and orange food coloring.

To make royal icing, follow these steps:

1. Confectioners' sugar and meringue powder. Stir in 1 1/2 tablespoons water until combined.

Liquid Web Cocktails

YIELDS:2

TOTAL TIME:0 hours 10 mins

INGREDIENTS

- 3 oz. liqueur de chocolate

- 3 ounces coffee liqueur (for example, Kahla)
- Milk, 2 oz.
- Whipped cream with a hint of sweetness
- Ice
- Nutmeg or pumpkin pie spice

DIRECTIONS

Combine the chocolate and coffee liqueurs, milk, whipped cream, and ice; mix until chilled. Using a strainer, pour into cocktail glasses. Sprinkle with pumpkin pie spice or nutmeg for garnish. Add little plastic spiders to the top.

Smokey Pumpkin Deviled Eggs

YIELDS: 12 servings

TOTAL TIME: 0 hours 35 mins

INGREDIENTS

- 1 dozen hard-boiled eggs
- 5 tbsp. pure pumpkin puree
- Mayonnaise, 3 tbsp.
- 1 tbsp. mustard Dijon
- 2 tsp. horseradish, prepared
- 1 teaspoon paprika, smoked
- Kosher salt and black pepper, freshly ground
- 6 petite cornichons

DIRECTIONS

1. Peel eggs and cut lengthwise in half. Remove yolks and reserve whites.

2. In a food processor, mix the yolks, pumpkin, mayonnaise, mustard, horseradish, and paprika until smooth, about 30 seconds. Season with salt and pepper.

3. Fill a big zip-top bag halfway with the yolk mixture. Make a 3/4-inch hole in one of the bag's corners. The filling should be piped into each egg white's well. With a damp finger, smooth the yolk mixture. With a fork, create ridges on the yolks.

4. Halve the cornichon lengthwise and then across to get 24 pieces. Create a stem for each yolk by inserting 1 cornichon at one end. Refrigerate for up to 2 hours, covered with a damp paper towel (if desired).

Hats and Bats Chocolate-Peanut Butter Tarts

YIELDS: 20 servings

TOTAL TIME: 3 hours 5 mins

INGREDIENTS

- 1/2 cup peanut butter, smooth
- 1 and a half cup confectioners' sugar
- Approximately 1/3 cup of tiny chocolate chips
- 2 cups all-purpose flour, spooned and smoothed, plus additional flour for the work surface
- 1/4 cup chocolate powder, unsweetened
- 3 tbsp. sugar, granulated
- 1 and 1/2 teaspoon kosher salt

- 1/2 cup cold unsalted butter
- 1 package (8 oz.) cold cream cheese, cubed
- White frosting purchased from a store
- Sanding sugar in a white, for decorating

DIRECTIONS

1. In a mixing bowl, combine peanut butter and confectioners' sugar until smooth and a dough forms. Incorporate chocolate chips.
2. Pulse flour, cocoa powder, granulated sugar, and salt three to four times in a food processor. Add butter and pulse 5–6 times until pea-sized butter. Pulse in 10-12 times until dough forms. (If needed, add 1–2 teaspoons water to help form the dough.) Wrap each part in plastic wrap and flatten. Refrigerate for at least one hour and up to two days.
3. Preheat oven to 350°F Oven 350F. Parchment paper two baking pans. Roll out dough to 1/8 inch thickness on a floured work surface. Cut shapes with a 3-inch witch hat and bat cookie cutters; arrange half of each shape on the prepared baking sheet, 1/2-inch apart. Fill the center with peanut butter, leaving a tiny boundary around the perimeter. Brush water around the borders and adhere to a duplicate cutout on top. With a fork, crimp the edges.
4. Bake 9 to 10 min, or until thoroughly cooked. Cool thoroughly on wire racks. Snip a very small hole in one corner of a ziptop bag and add a small amount of white frosting. Bats with pipe eyes and witch hats with a band. Sift sanding sugar over.

Spooky Forest Pudding Cups

YIELDS:10

TOTAL TIME:3 hours 50 mins

INGREDIENTS

- 1 and 1/2 cup sugar
- 1/2 cup chocolate powder, unsweetened
- 1 and a third cup cornstarch
- 1 teaspoon kosher salt
- 3 1/2 c. unsweetened condensed milk
- 6 big yolks of eggs
- 8 oz. chopped semisweet chocolate
- 4 tablespoons unsalted butter
- 4 tbsp. unsweetened pure vanilla extract
- 20 chocolate sandwich cookies in their entirety, plus 12 crushed
- 1 1/2 teaspoon chocolate candy melts
- bamboo skewers, 4 or 6 inches
- Optional chocolate sprinkles
- Candy pumpkins for decorative purposes

DIRECTIONS

1. Whisk together sugar, cocoa, cornstarch, and salt in a medium saucepan. Incorporate milk and eggs. Cook constantly whisking over medium heat until the mixture begins to bubble and thickens slightly 5 to 7 minutes. (Ensure that the bottom and inside corners of the pan are stirred often to avoid burning.) Take the pan off the heat. Combine the chocolate,

butter, and vanilla extract. Stir constantly until chocolate is melted and smooth.

2. Fill ten juice glasses halfway with 1 entire cookie (about 6 ounces each). Distribute half of the pudding equally on top. Add a second cookie on top. Distribute the remaining pudding evenly among the glasses. Distribute smashed cookies equally on top; cover and chill.

3. Place the tree template on a baking sheet beneath a sheet of parchment paper. Melt candy melts as directed. Transfer to a large ziptop bag with a strong zipper and cut a small hole in one corner. Pipe a line of molten chocolate along the tree trunks and insert the bamboo skewers. To build trees, pipe chocolate over the bamboo skewer and along the remaining lines on the template (this can be done loosely—there is no need to follow the design completely). Sprinkle chocolate sprinkles on the branches. Refrigerate until set.

4. Arrange chocolate trees in pudding glasses and garnish with candy pumpkins.

Towering Haunted House Cake

YIELDS: 30 servings

TOTAL TIME: 5 hours 0 mins

INGREDIENTS

For the Cake (Make Twice):

- 1 3/4 cup all-purpose flour, leveled with a spoon
- 2 c. sugar, granular
- 3/4 cup chocolate powder, unsweetened

- 2 tsp. bicarbonate of soda
- 1 and a half teaspoon baking powder
- kosher salt, 1 tsp.
- Three big eggs
- Approximately 2/3 cup vegetable oil
- 1 tsp. unsweetened pure vanilla extract
- 1 cup of warm milk

To make the Vanilla Buttercream and garnish:

- At room temperature, 2 1/2 cup unsalted butter (5 sticks)
- 7 1/2 cup confectioner's sugar, sifted
- 1 and a half teaspoon pure vanilla extract
- 1 kosher salt pinch
- 17 crushed and divided chocolate sandwich cookies
- Food coloring in black
- 1 cup candy melts in black
- Fondant noir
- Dust of silver luster
- fondant blanc
- Sprinkles of Wilton bones and skulls on the tops of windows and doors
- Sixlets in black and gray for roof and balcony
- Sprinkles of green for moss
- For plants, green licorice or sour strings
- Dragées in black and gunmetal for use above windows and doors, as well as along house corners
- Lollipops in silver and white for door trim

DIRECTIONS

Create a cake:

1. Preheat the oven to 350 degrees F. Grease and line the bottom of a 9-by-13-inch baking pan with parchment paper. Grease the parchment paper.
2. With an electric mixer on medium speed, whisk together flour, sugar, cocoa, baking soda, baking powder, and salt until mixed, about 1 minute. Combine the eggs, oil, vanilla, and milk in a medium mixing bowl. Whisk on low speed until smooth, approximately 1 minute. Increase to a medium speed and beat for two minutes.
3. Distribute the batter in the pan. Bake, rotating once, for 35 to 40 minutes, or until a toothpick inserted in the center comes out clean. Allow 15 minutes for cooling in the pan on a wire rack. Remove to a wire rack and cool fully. Construct a second cake. Wrap chilled cakes in plastic wrap and refrigerate for 1 hour to 2 days.

Prepare buttercream as follows:

1. With an electric mixer on speed, beat butter until smooth and creamy, about 1 to 2 minutes. Add confectioners' sugar, 1/2 cup at a time, beating well after each addition and scraping the bowl's sides as needed. Incorporate vanilla and salt. (Refrigerate for up to 1 week or use within 2 hours. Beat until smooth before using.)
2. Combine 1 2/3 cup buttercream and 10 crumbled cookies in a separate bowl. Transfer remaining buttercream to a ziptop bag and snip a small hole in one corner (or to a piping bag fitted with a color remaining buttercream gray with black food coloring; transfer 1 cup to a ziptop bag and snip a small hole in one corner).

3. Line a baking sheet with parchment paper and place the fence template on top. As directed on the packaging, melt black candy melts, transfer to a ziptop bag, and cut a small hole in one corner. Pipe melted candy onto parchment paper using the template as a guide; chill.

4. Cut cake following the template. On a platter, arrange 1 base layer; ice the top with approximately 2/3 cup cookie buttercream. Continue with the remaining base layer, icing only the left side. Frost second-story layer with about 1/3 cup frosting; top with remaining second-story layer. Assemble the tower pieces beside the second floor, frosting between the layers. Add roof pieces on top, frosting between layers. Outside, frost with gray buttercream. Create a siding texture with a cake comb.

5. Roll black fondant to a thickness of about 1/8-inch. Cut windows and doors using templates; gently press a butter knife into the windows to make panes. Lightly dust windows and doors with luster dust; adhere to the house. Roll black and white fondant together to create small marbled stones for the walkway.

6. Decorate the roof, windows, and entire exterior with candy, using the gray frosting in the piping bag as "glue." Combine with the Chocolate Fence. Create a path with the remaining seven crushed cookies.

Black-Bottom Brownies

YIELDS: 16 servings

TOTAL TIME: 1 hour 0 mins

INGREDIENTS

Brownies
- 3/4 cup unsalted butter, cubed, plus additional for pan
- 8 oz. chopped bittersweet chocolate
- 1 tsp. unsweetened pure vanilla extract
- 1 and 1/4 cup sugar
- 1/2 cup chocolate powder, unsweetened
- 1 and a half teaspoon instant espresso powder
- 1/4 tablespoon kosher salt
- 4 extra-large eggs
- 1 cup all-purpose flour, leveled with a spoon

Topping for cheesecake
- 8 oz. (1 box) room temperature cream cheese
- 1 big, room-temperature egg
- 2 tablespoons sugar
- 1 tsp. unsweetened pure vanilla extract

DIRECTIONS

1. heat oven 350°F and position a baking sheet on the center rack. Grease an 8-by-8-inch baking pan with butter. Line the bottom and sides of parchment paper, leaving a 2-inch overhang on two sides; butter paper.
2. Prepare the brownies: Melt butter in a medium saucepan over medium heat; remove from heat. Stir in chocolate until melted and smooth. Add vanilla extract. Stir in sugar until the mixture is smooth and glossy. Combine cocoa, espresso, and salt; set aside to cool for 10 minutes.

3. Continue whisking the eggs into the chocolate mixture until well integrated. Stir in flour until smooth. 1/4 cup batter; put aside. The rest of the batter should be transferred to the prepared pan.
4. To make the cheesecake topping, beat cream cheese on medium speed with an electric mixer until smooth, about 1 to 2 minutes. Reduce the mixer's speed. 30 seconds to 1 minute, beat in egg, sugar, and vanilla extract until completely combined, scraping down sides as required. Distribute evenly over brownie batter.
5. Using a butter knife, carefully swirl reserved chocolate batter on the cream cheese layer. Place the pan on top of the preheated baking sheet and bake for 35 to 40 min, or until a toothpick inserted in the center comes out with moist crumbs attached. Allow cooling in the pan on a wire rack.
6. Lift brownies off the pan using paper. Remove paper and cut brownies into shapes or 16 bars using a witch hat cookie cutter.

"Poison" Candy Apples

YIELDS:12
PREP TIME:0 hours 40 mins
TOTAL TIME:1 hour 0 mins

INGREDIENTS
- 12 Granny Smith baby apples
- 12 wooden dowels or candy apple sticks
- 1 and 1/2 cup sugar
- 1/2 cup corn syrup, light

- 1 tsp. food coloring black gel paste

DIRECTIONS

1. Thoroughly wash and dry apples. Arrange on a baking sheet and pierce with dowels firmly. Set aside a second baking sheet lined with buttered parchment paper.
2. Combine sugar, 3/4 cup water, and corn syrup in a medium saucepan. Over medium heat, stir until the sugar dissolves. Allow the temperature to rise without stirring until it reaches 310 degrees F, the hard-crack point. Take the pan off the heat. Remove thermometer carefully and apply food coloring.
3. Swirl the pan to completely incorporate the color. Swipe and spin the apple in the candy, shaking off excess and placing it on a prepared baking pan. Rep with the remainder of the apples.

Spiced Chocolate Bat Cookies

YIELDS: 1 dozen
PREP TIME: 0 hours 45 mins
TOTAL TIME: 2 hours 30 mins

INGREDIENTS

- 2 and 1/2 cup flour
- 1/2 cup cocoa powder
- 1/2 teaspoon cardamom powder
- 1/2 teaspoon cinnamon powder
- 1/2 teaspoon coarse sea salt
- 1 and a half teaspoon baking soda

- 1/2 tsp. baking powder
- 3/4 cup granulated dark brown sugar
- 1 and a half sticks of unsalted butter
- one huge egg
- 1/2 cup molasses, sulfured
- Edible silver sugar pearls
- sugar, granulated

DIRECTIONS

1. Whisk together the first 7 ingredients in a mixing basin until well blended; set aside.

2. In a large mixing basin, combine sugar and butter; beat with the paddle attachment of an electric mixer. Add egg and beat for about 4 minutes, or until pale and fluffy. Combine with molasses. Beat in flour mixture for 1 minute, until just combined.

3. Halve the dough. Roll each into a 3/8-inch-thick disk between two pieces of parchment paper. 1 hour in the refrigerator.

4. Preheat oven to 325 degrees Fahrenheit. Cocoa powder can be used to dust the countertop.

5. Transfer dough to a work surface and shape cookies using a 6-inch bat-shaped cutter (see note) or preferred size (adjust baking time accordingly). Rep with the remainder of the dough. On parchment paper-lined baking sheets, arrange 1 inch apart.

6. Bake for approximately 12 minutes, switching the baking pans halfway through or until the cookies are crisp. For eyes, lightly place two sugar pearls into each cookie. Allow 5 min for cookies to cool on baking pans before transferring them to a wire rack to cool entirely.

7. Lightly cover the tops of the bat wings with water using a pastry brush. Sprinkle sugar on top and leave aside.

Peanut Butter Acorns

YIELDS: 1 dozen
PREP TIME: 0 hours 15 mins
COOK TIME: 0 hours 10 mins
TOTAL TIME: 0 hours 35 mins

INGREDIENTS

- 3/4 cup natural peanut butter, smooth
- 3/4 cup confectioners' sugar
- 1 tsp. vanilla extract
- 1 extra-large egg
- 1 tablespoon flour
- 1 and a half cup mini chocolate chips
- 48 delicious chocolate kisses

DIRECTIONS

1. Preheat oven to 350°F. Beat the first 5 ingredients until smooth.
2. Spoon dough onto an unlined baking sheet in rounded 1/4 teaspoonfuls. Each component should be flattened into a dome form.
3. Bake for 10 min, or until the sides are golden, flipping the baking sheet halfway through. Allow 5 minutes for cooling on baking sheets.
4. In a small heat-proof bowl, microwave 1/4 cup of tiny chips on high for 30 seconds, stirring at 10-second intervals. Each chocolate kiss's bottom half should be dipped in melted chocolate and placed on the flat side of each

cookie. Affix a tiny chip "stem" to the top of each cookie using the same technique, completing the acorn.

Meringue Ghost Tartlets

YIELDS:8 servings
PREP TIME:2 hours 0 mins
COOK TIME:0 hours 20 mins
TOTAL TIME:2 hours 30 mins

INGREDIENTS

Graham Cracker Crust

- 8 oversized graham cracker planks (1 packet)
- 1 and a third cup sugar
- melted butter, 6 tbsp.

Ganache chocolate

- 1 tbsp. heavy cream
- 4 ounces bittersweet chocolate, chopped

Meringue Spirits

- 1 and 1/2 cup sugar
- 6 egg whites, big
- 1 heaping teaspoon cocoa powder

DIRECTIONS

1. Preheat the oven to 350 degrees F.
2. Crush Graham Crackers into small bits to form Graham Cracker Crust. Transfer to a food processor bowl; add sugar. Process until the crackers

have the consistency of a very fine crumb. Pulse in butter until combined.

3. Bake 20 min, or until the edges of the tartlets darken slightly, until the graham cracker mixture is uniformly distributed among 8 (2 1/2-inch) small pie pans. Allow cooling.
4. To prepare Chocolate Ganache, boil cream in a small saucepan over moderate heat until simmering. Remove from heat and stir in chocolate. Scoop into graham cracker crusts.

To make Meringue Ghosts, follow these steps:

1. In a saucepan over medium-high heat, heat 3 inches of water. Bring to a boil, then reduce heat. Sugar and egg whites in a heat-proof dish. Whisk the sugar and egg whites together in a basin set over the water. Stir frequently until sugar is dissolved and the mixture reaches a temperature of 212°F. (Rub a small amount between your fingertips. If the mixture is grainy, the sugar has not dissolved completely.)
2. Remove bowl from heat and beat egg white mixture with an electric mixer fitted with the whisk attachment until shiny, firm peaks form. Fill a disposable pastry bag halfway with meringue, snip the end to about 1 1/2 inches wide, and pipe 4-inch-tall ghost forms onto the ganache.
3. Shape the eyes and mouth with a little paintbrush dipped in cocoa. Serve right away.

Chocolate Pumpkin Witch Cupcakes

YIELDS: 12 servings
PREP TIME: 0 hours 40 mins

TOTAL TIME: 1 hour 30 mins

INGREDIENTS

Chocolate Pumpkin Cupcakes

- 1 tbsp. cocoa powder
- 1 cup unbleached all-purpose flour
- 3/4 tsp. bicarbonate of soda
- 3/4 teaspoon coarse sea salt
- 1/2 teaspoon cinnamon powder
- 1/2 tsp. ginger powder
- 1/8 teaspoon allspice, ground
- 1 and a third cup brown sugar
- 11 tbsp. softened unsalted butter
- three big eggs
- 3/4 cup pureed pumpkin
- 1 teaspoon extract de vanilla

Frosting with Hazelnut Cream Cheese

- Black candy melts, 6 oz.
- 12 sugar ice cream cones with pointed ends
- Cupcake liners on black paper

Frosting with Hazelnut Cream Cheese

- 1 box (8 oz.) cream cheese
- 2 unsalted butter sticks
- 1 tablespoon confectioners' sugar
- 1/4 cup chocolate hazelnut spread
- 1 tsp. vanilla extract

DIRECTIONS

1. Preheat the oven to 350 degrees F.
2. In a medium basin, whisk together the first seven ingredients. Cream sugar and butter in a mixing basin until light and fluffy with an electric mixer. Combine eggs and pumpkin puree. Add vanilla extract. Beat in flour mixture until fully mixed.
3. Prepare a 12-cup muffin tray by lining it with paper liners. Distribute mixture evenly among prepared muffin cups, filling each approximately 3/4 full.
4. A toothpick placed into one of the cupcakes comes out clean after 20-25 minutes.
5. Preheat oven to 350°F. Line a baking sheet with parchment paper. Microwave candy melts on high for 30 seconds, stirring every ten seconds. Cones are covered with candy melts by hand. Baking sheet dry. 1 3/4 inch hole in the center of a paper cupcake liner. Arrange atop candy-coated ice cream cone to create the witch's hat's brim.
6. Drizzle Hazelnut Cream Cheese Frosting over cupcakes. Each one should be topped with a witch's hat.
7. To create the Hazelnut Cream Cheese Frosting: Combine all ingredients in a large mixing basin. Lightly beat with an electric mixer's whisk attachment.

Cereal Bar Hay Bales

YIELDS:6

PREP TIME:0 hours 35 mins

TOTAL TIME: 0 hours 45 mins

INGREDIENTS

- 5 tbsp. butter, plus additional for the pan
- 2 (3-ounce) shredded wheat packets
- 15 ounces marshmallows (about 1 1/2 bags)
- 6 c. cereal puffed rice
- 6 laces licorice

DIRECTIONS

1. Butter an 8-inch square baking pan. In a bowl, crush shredded wheat to create fine splinters.
2. Melt butter in a pot over low heat. Stir in marshmallows until completely melted. Incorporate rice cereal. Toss with a rubber spatula to fully coat the cereal.
3. Scrape the mixture into the prepared pan, flattening it with the spatula.
4. Transfer cereal treats squares from pan to cutting board. Make a horizontal cut in half and then two evenly spaced vertical cuts to create six rectangles.
5. While the bars are still warm, sprinkle crushed shredded wheat on the sides. Each bale should be wrapped in licorice laces.

Almond Shortbread Owls

YIELDS: 2 dozen
PREP TIME: 0 hours 45 mins
COOK TIME: 0 hours 20 mins

TOTAL TIME: 2 hours 0 mins

INGREDIENTS

- 1 1/2 cup almonds, sliced
- 2 c. unbleached all-purpose flour
- One lemon's zest
- 1/2 teaspoon coarse sea salt
- 1 tablespoon unsalted butter
- 1 tablespoon confectioners' sugar
- 3/4 teaspoon extract almond
- 1/4 cup cocoa nibs
- 1/4 cup unsalted almonds
- 2 tbsp. sunflower seeds shelled

DIRECTIONS

1. Preheat oven to 350 degrees F. Grinds 3/4 cup of sliced almonds into a fine meal using a coffee grinder or food processor. Whisk together ground almonds, flour, zest, and salt in a large mixing basin.
2. In a large mixing basin, combine the butter, sugar, and extract and beat with an electric mixer until smooth. Stir in flour mixture until blended. Halve the dough. Each piece should be flattened into a 1/2-inch-thick slab and tightly wrapped in plastic wrap; chill for 1 hour or until firm.
3. Using a 2-1/2-inch diameter round cookie cutter, cut circles from the dough. Arrange 2 inches apart on baking pans coated with parchment paper. Make 1/4 teaspoon spherical dough balls for the eyes using scraps of dough. Two balls should be lightly pressed onto the top of each circle, and a whole almond should be placed on its side between them

for the beak. Each dough ball should have a chocolate chip for the pupil. To create the owls' toes, use sunflower seeds. For wings, overlap three sliced almonds on each side.

4. Bake for approximately 20 minutes, swapping baking sheets halfway through or until the cookies' edges are gently brown. Allow for approximately 5 minutes on the baking sheet before transferring to a wire rack to cool fully.

Brown Butter-Hazelnut Blondies

YIELDS:16 servings

PREP TIME:0 hours 25 mins

TOTAL TIME:2 hours 0 mins

INGREDIENTS

- 3/4 cup unsalted butter (1 1/2 sticks), plus additional for pan
- 1 1/2 cup all-purpose flour, leveled with a spoon
- 1 1/4 tsp. salt, kosher
- 1 tsp. bicarbonate of soda
- 1 1/2 cup dark brown sugar, packed
- 1 and a half teaspoon pure vanilla extract
- 2 extra-large eggs
- 1 1/2 cup toasted hazelnuts, finely chopped

DIRECTIONS

1. Preheat oven to 375 °F. Aluminum foil the bottom and sides of a 9-by-9-inch baking pan, allowing a 2-inch overhang on two sides; butter foil. In a bowl, combine flour, salt, and baking powder.

2. In a small saucepan over medium-high heat, cook butter, stirring, until aromatic and a deep golden brown color, about 6 to 8 minutes. Transfer to a bowl and set aside for 10 minutes to cool. Add sugar and vanilla extract. Add eggs whisking well after each addition. Incorporate flour mixture. Incorporate toasted hazelnuts. Transfer to the pan that has been prepared.

3. Bake for 24 to 26 minutes, or until a wooden pick inserted in the center comes out with a few moist crumbs attached. Allow cooling completely in the pan on the wire rack. Lift blondies from the pan using foil. Cut blondies into 16 squares after removing the foil.

Cookies Magnifying Glass Cookies

YIELDS:24

PREP TIME:1 hour 0 mins

TOTAL TIME:3 hours 0 mins

INGREDIENTS

- 2 1/4 c. all-purpose flour, spooned and smoothed, with additional flour for working
- 3/4 tsp. salt, kosher
- 3/4 cup unsalted butter
- 3/4 cup sugar
- 2 tbsp. unsweetened vanilla extract
- 1 and a half teaspoon pure almond essence

- 1 big beaten egg
- 1 cup crushed pineapple Lifesavers
- 1/2 cup green apple, finely crushed Candy Lifesavers

DIRECTIONS

1. In a mixing basin, whisk together flour and salt. With an electric mixer on medium speed, beat butter, sugar, and extracts until light and fluffy, about 1 to 2 minutes. Incorporate egg until well combined. Reduce mixer speed to low and add flour mixture to butter mixture in a slow, steady stream, mixing only until flour is absorbed.
2. Divide the dough in half and form two disks. Wrap with plastic wrap and place in the refrigerator for at least 2 hours or 3 days.
3. Preheat oven to 325 degrees Fahrenheit. Preheat oven to 350°F. Line three baking pans with parchment paper. Roll dough to a 1/4-inch thickness, one disk at a time, on a lightly floured work surface. Cut as many cookies as possible with a 5 3/4-inch-long magnifying glass-shaped cookie cutter; place on prepared baking pans. Remove the center of each cookie using a 2-inch round cutter; reroll scraps and continue the process. Freeze for ten minutes. In a bowl, combine candies.
4. Bake 10 to 12 min, or until the edges are golden brown. 3 minutes to cool. Distribute crushed candies evenly in the center of each cookie. Bake for 2 to 3 minutes, or until candies melt; swirl with a toothpick to combine colors. Allow cooling completely on a wire rack set over baking sheets.

Devil's Food Cupcakes

YIELDS:12

PREP TIME:1 hour 0 mins

TOTAL TIME:2 hours 0 mins

INGREDIENTS

- 1/4 cup chocolate powder, unsweetened
- 6 tbsp. strong coffee
- 1 1/4 cup all-purpose flour, leveled with a spoon
- 1/2 tsp. salt, kosher
- 1 and a half teaspoon baking powder
- 1/4 tsp. bicarbonate of soda
- 1 cup of sugar
- 1/2 cup (1 stick) room temperature unsalted butter
- At room temperature, 2 big eggs
- 1 tsp. unsweetened pure vanilla essence
- 1/2 cup room temperature sour cream
- 1 cup blue and yellow chocolate candies (such as M&M's or Sixlets), plus more candies for decoration
- Buttercream with cream cheese
- Food coloring in yellow

DIRECTIONS

1. heat oven 350 degrees F. Use paper liners to line a 12-cup standard muffin tray. Combine chocolate and coffee in a blender until smooth; set aside to chill. Whisk together flour, salt, baking powder, and baking soda in a mixing basin.

2. Beat sugar and butter on medium speed until light and fluffy, 2–4 minutes. Beat in eggs one at a time, until mixed. Add vanilla extract. Reduce mixer speed to low and whisk in flour mixture and sour cream alternately until flour is integrated, beginning and ending with flour mixture. Incorporate cocoa mixture.

3. Spoon batter evenly into the prepared tin. Toasted toothpick put in the center comes out clean after 24 to 26 minutes. Allow the tin to cool completely on a wire rack.

4. Scoop a hole in the top of each cupcake using a tablespoon measure. Fill equally with candies. 5. Using food coloring, tint Cream Cheese Buttercream to the desired shade, and frost cupcakes. Additional candies can be used to decorate.

Footprints Malted Sheet Cake

YIELDS: 12 - 16 servings
PREP TIME: 0 hours 30 mins
TOTAL TIME: 2 hours 30 mins

INGREDIENTS

Baking spray

- 4 1/2 cup cake flour, leveled with a spoon
- Approximately 2/3 cup malted milk powder
- 1 tbsp. baking powder
- 1 1/2 tsp. salt, kosher
- 2 and 1/4 cup sugar
- 1 1/2 cup unsalted butter (3 sticks), room temperature

- 5 medium-sized eggs, room temperature
- 1 tbsp. unsweetened pure vanilla extract
- 1 and a half cup buttermilk
- Buttercream with cream cheese
- For decoration, use a footprint template, cocoa powder, and Candy Pearls.

DIRECTIONS

1. Preheat oven to 325 °F. Spray a 9-by-13-inch baking pan. Whisk together flour, malted milk powder, baking powder, and salt in a mixing dish.

2. Beat sugar and butter on medium speed until light and fluffy, 4–6 minutes. Beat in eggs one at a time, until mixed. Add vanilla extract. Reduce mixer speed to low and whisk in flour mixture and buttermilk alternately until flour is integrated, beginning and ending with flour mixture.

3. Spoon batter into prepared pan. Bake for 55–1 hour, or until a toothpick inserted in the center comes out clean. Allow 15 minutes for cooling in the pan on a wire rack, then invert onto a rack to cool entirely.

4. Transfer cake to a serving tray and frost with Cream Cheese Buttercream; chill for 15 minutes. Dust cake with cocoa powder and place template on top. Distribute Candy Pearls evenly throughout the cake foundation.

Basic Sugar Cookie Dough

YIELDS:1

PREP TIME:0 hours 25 mins

TOTAL TIME:0 hours 25 mins

INGREDIENTS

- 2 3/4 cup all-purpose flour
- 1 and a half teaspoon baking powder
- Kosher salt, 1/4 tsp.
- 1 tablespoon unsalted butter
- 3/4 cup sugar, granulated
- 1 extra-large egg
- 1 and a half teaspoon pure vanilla extract

DIRECTIONS

1. Whisk the flour, baking powder, and salt in a large mixing bowl.

2. Beat the butter and sugar for 3 minutes until light and fluffy. Incorporate the egg and then the vanilla extract.

3. Reduce the mixer speed to low and add the flour mixture in a slow, steady stream, mixing until combined.

4. Preheat oven to 350 degrees F. 2 parchment-lined baking sheets. Cut out cookies with floured cookie cutters and arrange them on the prepared baking sheets. Reroll the scraps, chill, and cut them.

5. Bake, rotating the pans midway through until the edges of the cookies are softly golden brown, 10 to 12 minutes. Allow for 5 minutes on the sheets before transferring to wire racks to cool fully.

Apple-Cardamom Cakes with Apple Cider Icing

CAL/SERV:178

YIELDS:24 servings

PREP TIME: 0 hours 20 mins

TOTAL TIME: 0 hours 20 mins

INGREDIENTS

- 1/2 cup plus 2 teaspoons room temperature butter, plus additional for cake molds
- 2 1/4 cup all-purpose flour, plus additional flour to fill cake molds
- 1 tsp. bicarbonate of soda
- 1 teaspoon kosher salt
- 1 tsp. cardamom, ground
- Two eggs
- 1 and 1/2 cup sugar
- 1 1/2 teaspoon extract Vanilla
- 1 tablespoon applesauce
- 1/2 cup sour cream
- 1 1/2 teaspoon lemon zest
- 1 1/2 cup peeled and diced Apples Granny Smith
- Confectioners' sugar, 1 1/4 c.
- apple cider, 3 tbsp.

DIRECTIONS

1. Preheat oven to 400°F. Prepare 24 3 1/2-ounce cake molds or 2 12-cup cupcake tins by buttering and flouring them.
2. Sift together the flour, baking soda, salt, and cardamom.
3. Using a mixer set on medium-high speed, beat the eggs and sugar together being pulled from the basin, the mixture forms a thick ribbon. Reduce to a low speed and include the vanilla and applesauce. Beat in

1/2 cup melted butter, sour cream, and zest until well blended. Add the flour mixture in stages, mixing until smooth.

4. Fold the apples into the batter and distribute them evenly between the prepared molds (approximately 1/4 cup perform). Bake 20 to 25 min, or until a skewer inserted in the center of the cake comes out clean.

5. Cool 5 minutes on a wire rack. Remov the cakes from the molds and cool completely.

6. Make the glaze: In a bowl, whisk together the remaining melted butter, confectioners' sugar, and apple cider until smooth. Serve the cooled cakes with frosting.

7. Tip: While cardamom is a fragrant spice that matches beautifully with apples, this cake batter also works well with cinnamon, nutmeg, ginger, or all four spices. Experiment and personalize this cake to your liking.

Cookie Cutter Ginger Crisps

YIELDS:14 dozen
PREP TIME:0 hours 30 mins
COOK TIME:0 hours 0 mins
TOTAL TIME:1 hour 0 mins

INGREDIENTS

- 1 cup (2 sticks) softened butter
- 1 and a half cups brown sugar
- 1 and a half cups sugar
- 1 tbsp. molasses
- Approximately 2/3 cup light corn syrup

- 4 1/2 c. flour, sifted
- 1 1/2 tsp. cinnamon powder
- 1 1/2 tsp. ginger powder
- 1 teaspoon of salt
- 1 teaspoon of baking soda
- 1 and 1/2 teaspoon ground cloves

DIRECTIONS

1. heat oven 350 degrees F. Combine butter and sugars in a mixing bowl on a medium speed until light and fluffy. Combine molasses and corn syrup in a separate bowl until well blended. Continue stirring in the remaining ingredients until a smooth dough forms. Allow 30 minutes to chill.
2. Roll the dough to a thickness of less than 1/8 inch on a floured surface. Use floured cutters to cut. Bake for 8 minutes on a prepared cookie sheet.

Pumpkin Mousse

CAL/SERV:531

YIELDS:16

TOTAL TIME:8 hours 30 mins

INGREDIENTS

- 5 big yolks of eggs
- 1 cup of sugar
- 3 1/2 c. unsweetened condensed milk
- Canned pumpkin, 15 oz.
- 2 tsp. essence de vanilla

- 1 1/2 tsp. cinnamon powder
- 1/2 tsp. ginger powder
- 1/4 teaspoon freshly ground nutmeg
- 1 and 1/4 tsp. Salt
- two tbsp. dark rum
- 1 tsp. gelatin powder
- 3 oz. dark chocolate shavings

DIRECTIONS

1. Set aside a big basin halfway filled with ice water.

2. In a medium saucepan, whisk the yolks, 3/4 cup plus 2 tablespoons sugar, and 3/4 cup cream. Over medium-low heat, cook, constantly stirring with a rubber spatula or wooden spoon, until the mixture thickens and coats the spatula — about 10 minutes. Transfer to a medium bowl and place over an ice bath to chill. To cool, stir.

3. To the egg mixture, add pumpkin, vanilla, spices, and salt. In a small bowl, combine 1 tablespoon rum and 1 teaspoon gelatin. Stir in the remaining tablespoon of rum until dissolved. Whisk gently into the pumpkin mixture. 1/2 cup cream, beaten to firm peaks, should be folded into the pumpkin mixture. Fill a shallow dish halfway with water, cover, and refrigerate until cold and thick enough to fall in heavy dollops from a spoon — about 8 hours or up to overnight.

4. Whip the remaining cream and sugar to firm peaks using an electric mixer. Alternate layers of pumpkin mousse and whipped cream in a glass serving dish. Between the top two layers, sprinkle the chocolate shavings. Chill before serving.

Maple Cupcakes

CAL/SERV:222

YIELDS:18 servings

PREP TIME:0 hours 15 mins

TOTAL TIME:0 hours 45 mins

INGREDIENTS

- 2 1/2 tablespoons all-purpose flour
- 2 tsp. baking powder
- 1 tsp. bicarbonate of soda
- 1 and a half teaspoon salt
- 3/4 tsp. ginger powder
- 1 unsalted butter stick, softened
- 1/2 cup sugar, light-brown
- 2 extra-large eggs
- 1-and-a-quarter cup maple syrup
- 2 tsp. essence vanilla
- 1 and a half cups buttermilk
- 1/2 cup finely chopped walnuts
- Frosting with Maple-Butter

DIRECTIONS

Preheat oven to 350 degrees F. Combines the flour, baking powder, baking soda, salt, and ginger in a sifter. Place aside. In a large mixing basin, beat the butter and sugar together on medium speed until fluffy. Incorporate the eggs, syrup, and vanilla extract. By thirds, add the flour mixture, alternating with buttermilk. Add nuts. Fill 18 lined muffin cups halfway and bake for about 20 minutes, or until a tester comes out clean. Allow cooling completely. Frosted with maple-butter syrup.

Upside-Down Pear Tartlets

YIELDS: 6 servings
PREP TIME: 0 hours 20 mins
TOTAL TIME: 0 hours 50 mins

INGREDIENTS

- D'Anjou pears, 1 3/4 lb (about 4 medium pears)
- 4 tablespoons butter
- 1 cup of sugar
- 1 sheet puff pastry (8 by 10-inch) (about 8.5 ounces)

DIRECTIONS

1. Preheat oven to 400 °F. Pears should be peeled, cored, and sliced into 1/2-inch wedges. In a skillet, melt half the butter. Cook over medium-high heat, occasionally stirring, until pears release their juices and begin to turn golden around the edges. Drain the juices from the pears and set them aside.
2. In a large skillet, cook sugar over high heat until it melts, bubbles, and becomes amber. Add the 2 tsp of butter and pears, taking care not to stumble the caramel. Using a heatproof rubber spatula, turn to coat the

pears. Remove skillet from heat and pour pear slices into jumbo muffin tin cups (3/4-cup capacity). Arrange in a way that creates a 1-inch layer.

3. Cut the pastry into six 2 1/2-inch rounds (it should be approximately 1/8-inch thick). Scraps may be discarded or saved for another purpose. Bake until the puff pastry puffs and the pears are golden brown, about 25 minutes. Allow cooling on a wire rack.
4. Use a spoon to run around the perimeter of each tartlet. Remove from the oven and serve pear side up. Serve immediately.

Sweet Popcorn Balls

YIELDS:12 servings
PREP TIME:0 hours 20 mins
TOTAL TIME:1 hour 20 mins

INGREDIENTS

- Popped popcorn 1/2 tbsp.
- 3 c. dried fruit mixture, including golden raisins, cherries, chopped apricots, and figs
- 1 and a quarter cup granulated sugar
- 3/4 cup granulated sugar
- 1 tablespoon corn syrup
- 1/2 cup of water

DIRECTIONS

1. In a large, lightly oiled, heatproof bowl, combine popcorn and dried fruit. Oil 2 baking pans lined with waxed paper and a long metal fork Place aside.
2. In a saucepan fitted with a candy thermometer, bring sugar, brown sugar, corn syrup, and water to a boil over medium-high heat. Reduce heat to medium and simmer until 260°F.
3. Pour the syrup carefully over the popcorn mixture. To distribute, use a fork to stir. Allow sitting for 1–2 minutes.
4. Using well-oiled hands, shape 3-inch balls and lay them on prepared baking sheets to cool fully. Refrigerate for up to 4 days in an airtight container.

Marbled Chocolate Bark

CAL/SERV:358

YIELDS:8

PREP TIME:0 hours 15 mins

TOTAL TIME:4 hours 0 mins

INGREDIENTS

- Eight ounces of semisweet chocolate
- White chocolate, 8 oz.
- 1/2 cup almonds, sliced
- 1/2 cup cranberries, dried

DIRECTIONS

1. Preheat oven to 350°F. Line a baking sheet with nonstick foil. In two microwaveable bowls, warm chocolates on high for 2 minutes, swirling once or twice, until almost melted. Allow 1 minute before stirring until thoroughly melted and smooth.

2. Spoon melted chocolates alternately onto the prepared baking sheet and smooth out into a 14 × 10-inch rectangle using a spatula. Swirl chocolates together with an offset spatula to produce a marbled look. Almonds and cranberries should be equally distributed over chocolate. Allow to stand until stiff and set at room temperature (or refrigerate for 1 hour). Divide into huge chunks.

Turtle Corn

YIELDS: 15 servings
PREP TIME: 0 hours 40 mins
TOTAL TIME: 0 hours 40 mins

INGREDIENTS

- 16 c. unsalted fresh-popped popcorn
- 1 and a half teaspoon salt
- 8 oz. chopped dark baking chocolate
- 1 tsp. shortening (vegetable)
- 1 cup of sugar
- 1 c. corn syrup, light
- 1 cup heavy cream
- 1/4 pound butter, plus 2 tsp

DIRECTIONS

1. Butter an 11-by-17-inch baking pan with 2 teaspoons. Toss the popcorn and salt together and spread evenly across the bottom of the baking pan. Place aside.

2. In a double boiler or a heatproof dish, put over a saucepan of simmering water, and combine the chocolate and vegetable shortening, occasionally stirring until melted. Set aside and maintain a warm temperature.

3. Combine the sugar, corn syrup, cream, and butter in a medium saucepan. Bring the mixture to a simmer and continue cooking until the caramel reaches the firm-ball stage and a candy thermometer registers 249°F. Remove from the pan immediately and drizzle the caramel over the popcorn in fat ribbons.

4. Allow the caramel to cool completely. Over the popcorn, drizzle the chocolate in fat ribbons, taking care not to fully cover the caramel. Allow it cool completely before slicing into three-quarter-inch squares. Store for up to 3 days in an airtight container.

Peanut butter monsters

Yield: 30 peanut butter monsters
Prep time: 30 minutes
Total time: 30 minutes

Ingredients

- 6 tbsp. softened butter
- 1/2 cup peanut butter, creamy

- 1/4 cup marshmallow cream
- 1 teaspoon vanilla extract
- a sprinkle of salt
- 2 c. confectioners' sugar
- 1 bag of candy melts in green
- 30 oversized candy eyes
- purple sprinkles

Instructions

1. In a mixing bowl, cream the butter, peanut butter, marshmallow, vanilla extract, and salt until smooth.
2. Beat in the powdered sugar gradually. 30 evenly sized balls from the mixture. Refrigerate for at least an hour.
3. Melt the candy melts as directed. Then dip them in the melted candy using a toothpick. Remove the toothpick and place it on a piece of parchment paper. Cover the hole with the toothpick and slide it across the melted candy to produce a fur look.
4. Attach a candy eye to the front and sprinkle sprinkles on top. Allow setting.

Chocolate Peanut Butter Bars

Prep Time 20 MINUTES
Cook Time 10 MINUTES
Total Time 30 MINUTES
Servings: 16 bars

Ingredients

- 1 tbsp honey
- 1 tbsp pure maple syrup
- 1 cup luscious peanut butter
- 6 c. corn flakes
- 8-12 ounces melted semi-sweet or dark chocolate
- 6 oz. melted white chocolate 7. black sprinkles for decoration (optional)

Instructions

1. preheat oven to 350°F. Parchment paper a 9x13 baking pan.

2. Melt the honey, maple syrup, and peanut butter in a large microwave-safe bowl until smooth, about 30 seconds to 1 minute. Toss in the corn flakes until fully combined. Distribute the mixture evenly into the prepared pan, packing it firmly.

3. Melt the chocolate chips and distribute the melted chocolate evenly over the bars.

4. To construct the ghosts. Melt the white chocolate and then spoon a small dollop (1 teaspoon for little ghosts, 1 tablespoon for large ghosts) onto the chocolate, spacing each ghost 1 inch apart. Gently draw the white chocolate into a ghost form using a wooden stick or the point of a slender spoon; don't stress about making these perfect; the more flawed they seem, the better.

5. Use two little sprinkles or additional melted chocolate to create eyes.

6. Refrigerate the bars for 1 hour or until set. Cut around the ghost with a sharp knife, creating irregular forms. Refrigerate until ready to serve. BOO!

Bloody Truffles

PREP TIME 1 hr

CHILLING TIME 1 hr

TOTAL TIME 1 hr

YIELD 36 truffles

- **INGREDIENTS**
- 1 box cake mix, any flavor, baked as directed on the package
- 1 c. prepared to ice
- 48 Amarena cherries, if desired
- 24 oz white confectioner's sugar
- Embellished royal icing blades, axes, or other edible weapons
- Food coloring gel with the color red

PERSONALIZATION: 36

INSTRUCTIONS

1. Baking the cake mix in a 9x13-inch baking dish. Allow the cake to cool completely after baking.
2. In a mixing bowl, crumble the cake with your hands until it is in small pieces.
3. Transfer three-quarters of the frosting to a mixing bowl and stir with a rubber spatula until fully mixed. It moist and hold together when a cake ball is squeezed between your fingers, but not excessively moist or oily. If the cake mixture remains slightly dry and crumbly, add additional frosting to achieve the appropriate consistency—the precise amount will depend on the texture of the cake you started with.
4. Scoop out 1-inch balls of cake with a small cookie or candy scoop and roll between your palms until they are spherical. This recipe should yield approximately 36 balls.

5. **Cherry Variation:** To make a cherry filling, rinse and gently pat dry 48 Amarena cherries. Flatten a ball of cake truffle mix on your palm and center it with a cherry. Gently squeeze the cake mixture around the cherry and roll it between your palms to cover it entirely.
6. Place the cake balls on a parchment or waxed paper-lined baking sheet and refrigerate until solid for at least 1 hour. Additional time is OK, and even overnight is acceptable.
7. In a medium microwave-safe bowl, microwave the candy coating until melted, stirring every 30 seconds to prevent overheating.
8. Dip or fork a cake ball in the melted candy coating. Remove it from the coating and let any remaining liquid trickle into the dish. Replenish the baking sheet with the dipped truffles. Firmly push a royal icing knife or axe into the truffle while the coating is wet. Repeat with the remaining truffles until they are all dipped and decorated.
9. Once all of the cake balls have been dipped, chill the candies for about 20 minutes to properly set the coating. With a clean paintbrush, color the royal icing decorations on the truffles red.
10. Serve cold or refrigerate for up to a week.

Jack Skellington Cheesecakes

Prep Time 30 mins
Cook Time 15 mins
Total Time 45 mins
Servings: 18

Ingredients

Crust:

- 2 cups graham cracker crumbs, chocolate
- 5 tbsp granulated light brown sugar
- 8 teaspoons melted butter

Cheesecake Filling:

- 16 oz. 2 blocks softened cream cheese
- Approximately 2/3 cup sugar
- 2 extra-large eggs
- Approximately 2/3 cup sour cream
- 1 tsp vanilla extract or paste vanilla

Ganache chocolate:

- 3 oz. bittersweet chocolate, finely chopped or chips
- 3 tbsp heavy cream

Instructions

1. Preheat oven to 350 degrees F.
2. Combine the chocolate graham cracker crumbs, brown sugar, and melted butter in a medium mixing bowl.
3. Spoon roughly 2 tablespoons of the crumbs into 18 muffin cups lined with parchment paper.
4. Beat cream cheese on medium speed until creamy and smooth, scraping down the bowl as needed.
5. Beat in sugar until light and fluffy.
6. Beat in the egg and vanilla extract until creamy.
7. Gently fold in the sour cream.
8. Divide the cheesecake filling evenly among the 18 muffin cups, spooning about 2 tablespoons into each cup.

9. Bake for 15-18 minutes on the middle rack of the oven, or until the cheesecakes no longer appear wet, but the center still jiggles.

10. Take out of oven and cool.

11. Allow approximately an hour for cooling.

12. In a small glass measuring cup, combine chocolate and heavy whipping cream.

13. Microwave on high for 40 seconds.

14. Microwave the cup for 3 minutes, then remove and stir until melted.

15. If necessary, continue heating for ten additional seconds of power, stirring after each until dissolved.

16. Allow the chocolate ganache to cool somewhat before using.

17. Fill a pastry bag or squeeze bottle fitted with a #3 round tip with the mixture.

18. Decorate each cheesecake with two eyes, two noses, and a mouth to resemble Jack Skellington.

Notes on the Recipe

1. Refrigerate or freeze cheesecakes in an airtight container for up to 5 days or 3 months.

2. If you're bringing cheesecakes to a party where they'll be exposed to room temperature for an extended period, I recommend freezing them and transporting them frozen. Once left on the table, the cheesecakes will defrost in around 20 minutes and remain cool for longer than if you set our refrigerated cheesecakes out.

MUMMY COOKIES RECIPE

Prep Time 5 minutes
Cook Time 10 minutes
Refrigerate 30 minutes
Total Time 45 minutes
Servings 26

Ingredients

- 26 vanilla Vienna Fingers cookies
- 2 bags of white candy coating
- 52 Mini M&Ms

Instructions

1. Begin by melting candy coating according to the package directions.
2. Dip the cookie into melted candy using a fork, coating all sides. Rep with the remaining cookies on greased paper.
3. Allow candy coating to set (half an hour in the refrigerator or at least 1 hour on the counter).
4. Melt more candy coating in a microwave and place in a Ziploc bag. Snip the edge and drizzle the glaze over the cookies. As eyes, use small M&Ms. Allow setting. ENJOY!

Halloween Popcorn Balls

Prep Time: 15 min
Cook Time: 15 min
Additional Time: 30 min
Total Time: 1 hour
Servings: 8 -10 balls

Ingredients

- 16 cups of freshly popped popcorn, approximately 1 standard-size popcorn bag
- Mini marshmallows, 10 ounce
- 12 stick butter 1/4 cup
- 1 package Wilton candy melts in bright white
- cotton candy eyeballs I used standard-size ones.

Instructions

1. Combine the popcorn and butter (or 2 large bowls to make mixing easier).
2. Melt the micro marshmallows and butter in a large saucepan over medium heat. Occasionally stir until smooth.
3. Distribute the melted mixture evenly over the popcorn (dividing between 2 bowls if you divided the popcorn). With a spatula, stir until the popcorn is evenly coated.
4. Begin by buttering your hands and forming the popcorn into balls. You can create taller balls in the shape of a ghost or any other shape you desire.
5. Place the balls on a parchment or silicone-lined baking sheet. Allow for cooling and firming of the balls. (30–1 hour)
6. Melt the white candy melts as directed. If desired, you may add vegetable shortening or vegetable oil to thin the chocolate. Dip the popcorn balls' tops into the melted chocolate and place them back on the baking sheet. Allow 1-2 minutes for the chocolate to harden before adding sugar eyeballs to each ball. You can attempt to immediately add the eyeballs, but they may fall off if the chocolate is too hot.

7. Before serving, allow the chocolate to set. Place them in a Tupperware container if you intend to serve them the following day.
8. You can creatively show them! You can arrange them in a huge tray over Halloween-themed M&Ms and some fake spiders!

Double Chocolate Cookie Bark

YIELDS:10 servings

TOTAL TIME:1 hour 0 mins

Ingredients

For cookie

- 3/4 cup unbleached all-purpose flour
- 1/3 cup cocoa powder, unsweetened
- 1/4 tsp. bicarbonate of soda
- Kosher salt, 1/4 tsp.
- 4 tablespoons unsalted butter, room temperature
- 1 tbsp. sugar
- 1 extra-large egg
- 1 tsp. unsweetened pure vanilla extract

For topping

- 1 pound chopped white chocolate
- Candy-colored eyes

Directions

1. Whisk together flour, cocoa powder, baking soda, and salt in a medium bowl. In a large mixing bowl, beat butter and sugar with an electric mixer until light and fluffy, about 3 minutes. Incorporate the egg and

then the vanilla extract. Reduce mixer speed to low and slowly add flour mixture, mixing until incorporated.

2. Roll dough 2 sheets of parchment paper to about 1/8 inch. Slide dough onto the prepared baking sheet (remove and discard parchment paper) and chill for at least 20 minutes, or until firm.
3. heat oven 350 degrees F. Bake for 15 to 20 minutes, rotating baking sheet halfway through, or until cookie is set and darker around the edges. Allow to completely cool on a wire rack.
4. Once cooled, add white chocolate to a microwave-safe bowl and microwave in 30-second increments, stirring between each one, until melted and smooth. Spread the remaining 1/4 cup on top of the cookie. Allow setting.
5. Remelt remaining chocolate and drizzle over the top; before setting, if desired, add candy eyes. Allow setting. Before serving, cut or break into pieces.

Meringue Ghost Tarts

YIELDS:6 servings

TOTAL TIME:0 hours 40 mins

Ingredients

For tart shells

- Chocolate wafer cookies, 7 oz (we used Nabisco Famous Wafers)
- 6 tbsp. melted unsalted butter
- 6 small tart pans with removable bottoms (4.5 to 4.75 in.

For purposes of filling

- 8 oz. chopped semisweet chocolate
- 1 cup unsweetened condensed milk
- 4 tablespoons unsalted butter, room temperature
- 1/2 cup caramel sauce, prepared (optional)
- 12 chocolate chips, mini

For the sake of ghosts
- 2 huge egg whites.
- Approximately 2/3 cup granulated sugar
- 1 tablespoon cream of tartar

Directions

To make tart shells, pulse cookies in a food processor until fine crumbs appear. Pulse in melted butter until evenly coated; the mixture should retain its shape when squeezed. Divide mixture evenly across tart pans and press into corners, upsides, and bottom. Refrigerate for at least 10 minutes before serving.

Prepare the filling: In a medium bowl, place chocolate. In a saucepan over medium heat, heat cream until little bubbles form around the sides of the pan. Allow 1 minute for the cream to rest on top of the chocolate. Stir until the chocolate is completely melted, then add the butter and stir until completely melted. Spoon 1 tablespoon caramel into each tart shell if used. Divide chocolate mixture evenly between shells (about 1/3 cup per shell) and chill for 1 hour, or until ready to serve.

Construct meringue ghosts: Bring a medium pot to a boil with 1 inch of water. Add egg whites, sugar, 1/4 cup water, and cream of tartar to a large mixing basin. Place the bowl on the saucepan (ensuring that the bottom does not touch the water). Beat mixture with an electric mixer until stiff peaks form, about 5 minutes. Remove from heat and continue pounding for approximately 2 minutes, or until mixture cools.

Spoon little mounds of meringue onto tarts and swoop the spoon through the mixture. Serve immediately with additional meringue and small chocolate chips for the eyes. Remove from pans immediately before serving.

Candied Clementines

YIELDS:25

TOTAL TIME:3 hours 50 mins

Ingredients

For clementines

- 1 and 1/2 cup sugar
- 4 finely cut tiny clementines

To make ganache

- Bittersweet chocolate, 8 oz., finely chopped
- 3/4 cup unsweetened condensed milk

Directions

1. Heat sugar and 1 1/2 cups water in a medium skillet over low heat until sugar dissolves. Cook for 1 hour with clementine segments.
2. Preheat the oven to 200 degrees Fahrenheit. Transfer clementines to a baking sheet fitted with a nonstick liner and bake for about 2 1/2 hours, flipping twice. Allow cooling.

3. Once cooled, prepare the ganache: Combine chocolate and butter in a medium bowl. Gently heat heavy cream in a small saucepan over medium heat, then pour over chocolate. Allow 10 minutes before stirring until completely melted and smooth. Half of each clementine slice should be dipped in chocolate, then returned to the baking sheet to harden, about 1 hour.

Cookie Bat Cupcakes

YIELDS: 2 dozen

Ingredients

- Cupcakes de chocolate
- Buttercream Vanilla
- Gel food coloring can be used to tint icing.
- Miniature chocolate peanut butter cups (such as Reeses)
- Thin Chocolate Sandwich Cookies (such as Oreos)
- Icing Royale
- Eyeballs made of candy
- Toothpicks

Directions

1. Bake cupcakes as directed and cool thoroughly. Buttercream should be prepared and tinted to desired hues.
2. Using toothpicks, gently skewer chocolate peanut butter cups. Twist chocolate sandwich cookie thins in half; scrape the cream from the center and discard. Cut each cookie in half and glue the cookie "wings"

and candy eyeballs to the chocolate peanut butter cup "body" using royal icing.

Red Velvet Cookies

YIELDS:30

TOTAL TIME:0 hours 45 mins

Ingredients

- 1 and a half cups all-purpose flour
- 1/2 cup cocoa powder, Dutch-process
- 1 tsp. bicarbonate of soda
- 1 tsp. salt, kosher
- 1 cup (2 sticks) room temperature unsalted butter
- 3/4 cup brown sugar, packed
- 1/2 cup sugar, granulated
- a single huge egg
- 1 tsp. food coloring red gel paste
- Pure vanilla essence, 2 tsp.
- 1 pkg semisweet chocolate chips, 12 ounce

Directions

1. Preheat oven to 350°F Oven 350F. Parchment paper baking pans Large mixing bowl with flour, cocoa, baking soda, and salt
2. Beat butter and sugars together on a medium speed with an electric mixer until blended. Combine the egg, food coloring, and vanilla extract until barely mixed.

3. Reduce mixer speed to low and add flour mixture in a slow, steady stream until incorporated. Chocolate chunks should be folded in.
4. Place heaping spoonfuls of dough on prepared baking sheets, 1 1/2 inches apart.
5. Bake cookies until darker around the edges, 9 to 12 minutes total, turning pans on racks halfway through.
6. After 5 minutes, remove parchment (and cookies) to a wire rack to cool for 5 minutes before serving.

Moss Cookies

YIELDS: 3 dozen

TOTAL TIME: 0 hours 40 mins

Ingredients

- 1 cup all-purpose flour
- 1 and a half teaspoon baking powder
- 1 cup (2 sticks) room temperature unsalted butter
- 3/4 cup sugar, granulated
- Gel food coloring in moss and leaf green
- 1 extra-large egg
- 1 tbsp. unsweetened vanilla extract
- 1/2 cup buttercream or store-bought icing
- Graham crackers, 2

Directions

1. heat oven 350 degrees F and line two large cookie sheets with reusable silicone baking mats or parchment paper.
2. Whisk flour, baking powder, and salt in a large mixing bowl. In a separate large mixing basin, beat butter and sugar with an electric mixer until light and fluffy, about 3 minutes. Last minute dark green gel food coloring drops. Incorporate the egg and then the vanilla extract.
3. Reduce mixer speed to low and add flour mixture in a slow, steady stream, mixing just until combined. Using an offset spatula or the palm of your hand, distribute unevenly sized portions of dough into thin, rough cookie shapes (approximately 1/8 inch to 1/4 inch thick) on prepared cookie sheets.
4. Bake, changing pans halfway through, until the tops of the cookies feel sandy, 13 to 15 minutes. Allow cooling completely on a wire rack.
5. To add color to the icing, color it green. Graham crackers and 2 moss cookies should be finely crumbled. Working one at a time, put a thin coating of frosting on the underside of the remaining cookies and immediately sprinkle with cookie crumbs.

Halloween Snack Mix

YIELDS: 10 servings

TOTAL TIME: 0 hours 25 mins

Ingredients

- 9 c. cereal Rice Chex
- 1/2 cup almond butter, creamy
- Unsalted butter, 4 tbsp.

- 2 1/2 cup split semisweet chocolate chips
- 1.5 tsp pure vanilla extract
- Salt kosher
- 2 tablespoons confectioners' sugar
- 1/2 c. candy eyeballs

Directions

1. In a bowl, combine cereal and milk; leave aside.
2. Combine almond butter, butter, and 1 cup of chocolate chips in a separate large microwave-safe bowl. Microwave in 15-second intervals at 50% power, stirring in between, until melted and smooth.
3. Add vanilla extract and 1/2 teaspoon salt. Drizzle over cereal and toss to coat evenly.
4. Add half of the cereal mixture and half of the sugar to a resealable gallon-size bag. Shake and seal until every cereal is coated evenly.
5. Continue with the remaining cereal and sugar in the same bag. Combine the remaining 1.5 cups of chocolate chips and candy eyes in a separate bowl.

Spiderweb Cake

YIELDS:16 - 20 servings
TOTAL TIME:2 hours 0 mins

Ingredients

For cake

- Oil for frying pans

- 2 3/4 cup unbleached all-purpose flour
- 1 cup cocoa powder, black
- 1 cup sugar, granulated
- 1 cup granulated sugar
- 2 tsp. baking powder
- 1/2 tsp. bicarbonate of soda
- 1 tablespoon kosher salt
- Three big eggs
- 1 cup reduced-fat buttermilk
- 3/4 cup neutral oil, for example, canola
- 1 tsp. unsweetened pure vanilla essence
- 1 cup freshly prepared coffee

For icing

- 2 1/2 tbsp unsalted butter, room temperature
- 5 1 and a half cup confectioners' sugar
- kosher salt, 1 tsp.
- 1/4 to 1/3 cup room temperature heavy cream
- Food coloring gel in black
- 4 chocolate sandwich cookies, lightly crushed

To be used with spiders and webs

- 4 oz. finely chopped dark chocolate
- Sixlets candies in black

<u>Directions</u>

1. Preheat oven to 325 °F. Grease and parchment paper three 8-inch cake pans.

2. Sift flour and cocoa powder into a mixing basin. Combine sugars, baking powder, baking soda, and salt in a large mixing bowl.
3. Whisk together the eggs, buttermilk, oil, and vanilla extract until nearly incorporated. Add coffee gradually, constantly whisking, until smooth.
4. Bake 28-32 min, or until a wooden pick inserted in the center comes out clean. Invert pans onto wire racks for 10 minutes to cool thoroughly. Once cool, wrap cakes in a thin layer of plastic wrap and chill for 30 min or up to 1 day before decorating.

Make icing:
1. In a mixing bowl fitted with an electric stand mixer fitted with the paddle attachment, beat butter, sugar, and salt on low speed until completely incorporated. Increase speed to medium and beat for approximately 3 minutes, or until fluffy. Add cream gradually until a spreadable consistency is reached and beat until fluffy, about 3 minutes.
2. To assemble, lay 1 cake on a cake board or serving platter, flat side up. Spread 3/4 cup frosting evenly across the top of the cake, all the way to the edges. Repeat with the second cake layer, rounded side down. Continue with the final layer, rounded side up or down. Coat the entire cake with a thin coating of frosting and chill for at least 10 minutes, or until the frosting has set.
3. In a small dish, color 1/2 cup of remaining icing black. Set away in a piping bag fitted with a little round tip.
4. Fold broken cookies into remaining frosting; avoid over-mixing to prevent icing from becoming gray. Spread a thick layer of icing evenly over the cake and smooth with an offset spatula. Any remaining icing can adhere spiders and webs to the cake.

5. Sketch or print a spiderweb pattern to create spiders and webs and adhere it to your work surface. Place waxed paper over the top and secure corners with tape. Microwave two-thirds of the chocolate in 30-second increments on 50% power, stirring between each, until melted and smooth. Stir in the remaining chocolate until melted.

Create a piping bag as follows:

1. Begin by folding one corner of a large sheet of parchment paper over until the edges line up to form a triangle. Remove and discard any surplus. With the folded side facing you, bring the bottom right corner up to meet the triangle's top point, folding the paper inward to align. Using one hand to hold the points together, use the other to wrap the final point around to connect the points. Points should be folded into the piping bag.
2. Fill the bag halfway with melted chocolate and seal by folding the open end. Reduce the point of the piping tip to a little point and trace webs onto waxed paper. Allow to fully set before transferring to cake.
3. To create spiders, use black Sixlets candies and black icing to pipe legs. Allow to fully set before transferring to cake.

Halloween Cake Pops

YIELDS: 16

Ingredients

- 2 c. crumbs cake
- 1/2 cup buttercream or store-bought icing
- 1 1/2 pound white candy melts or finely chopped dark chocolate

- Coconut oil (1 tbsp per 8 oz candy melts)*
- Craft sticks made of wood
- For decorating, corn syrup, red gel food coloring, and fondant

Directions

1. Combine cake crumbs and frosting in a large mixing basin.

2. To embellish: Melt 8 oz candy melts and 1 tbsp coconut oil in a medium bowl in 30-second increments until melted and smooth. In a second dish, place two-thirds of the chocolate and microwave at 50% power in 30-second increments, stirring until melted and smoSpoon To coat the sides of the pop molds with melted chocolate, use the back of a spoon to spread it out evenly. Refrigerate for approximately 5 minutes or until hard. Insert wooden craft sticks halfway into molds and coat the sides with additional chocolate or melts. Allow setting.

3. Take out the sticks. Fill each pop with 1 tbsp cake mix, leaving a gap between the top of the mold and the stick, then gently re-insert the sticks. Add an extra 1 tablespoon of melted chocolate or candy melts and smooth and scrape away any excess with a little offset spatula. Refrigerate for approximately 5 minutes or until completely set. Remove each pop carefully, pressing the stick through the mold and further into the pop once it is completely gone. Rep the previous procedures to create 16 pops.

4. To make blood, add 1 teaspoon of corn syrup and a few drops of red gel food coloring in a small bowl. Arrange cake pops in a single layer on a big parchment paper. Splatter onto the completed cake pops using a wooden skewer.

5. In the case of the skeletal hand: Cornstarch dust silicone skeleton hand mold** lightly. Fill cavities with fondant and then use a small rolling pin to roll back and forth over the fondant until the excess is eliminated. Remove one finger at a time with caution. Apply a small amount of melted chocolate to the cake pop to secure it.

6. Prepare a piping bag for the chocolate spiders. Fold one corner of a large piece of parchment paper over until the edges line up to form a triangle. Remove and discard any surplus. With the folded side facing you, bring the bottom right corner up to meet the triangle's top point, folding the paper inward to align. Using one hand to hold the points together, use the other to wrap the final point around to connect the points. Points should be folded into the piping bag.

7. Fill the bag halfway with melted chocolate and seal by folding down the open end. Reduce the tip of the piping tip to a little point and pipe spiders directly onto the pops.

Black Cat Cookies

YIELDS: 1 dozen

Ingredients

- Simple Sugar Cookies
- Cookies with Black Cocoa
- Icing Royale
- Vodka or another clear alcoholic beverage
- Lustrous black and silver dust

Directions

1. Prepare cookie doughs according to package directions. Cut circles from sugar cookie dough using flour-coated circle cutters and cats from black cocoa cookie dough using cocoa-coated cat cutters. Bake as directed on package and cool thoroughly.
2. Decorate sugar cookies with royal icing and place cat cookies on top.
3. Using a small amount of clear alcohol and silver luster dust, paint small brushstrokes on the sugar cookies with royal icing. Rep with black luster dust to finish painting the bats.

Chocolate Skeleton Cookie Cupcakes

YIELDS: 2 dozen

Ingredients

- Cupcakes Vanilla
- Buttercream Vanilla
- Small pink, yellow, or green candies (such as Nerds)
- Cookies with Chocolate Skeleton

Directions

1. Bake cupcakes as directed and cool thoroughly. Vanilla buttercream is used to frost the cake, coated in candies.
2. bake and decorate cookies according to the directions. Once completely dried, press into candy-coated cupcakes.

Frankenstein Cake

YIELDS: 10 servings

TOTAL TIME: 2 hours 15 mins

Ingredients

For each cake

- Butter and 1 tbsp. flour for the pan
- 2 cups unbleached all-purpose flour
- 1 teaspoon baking powder
- 1 teaspoon kosher salt
- 1 cup (2 sticks) room temperature unsalted butter (divided)
- 1/4 cup unbleached dark brown sugar
- 1 tbsp. cinnamon powder
- 1 and a quarter cup granulated sugar
- 3 large eggs, room temperature
- 1/2 cup whole milk, room temperature
- 1 tsp. unsweetened pure vanilla extract

For icing

- 1/2 cup unsalted butter
- 4 tbsp. (1/4 cup) cream cheese, room temperature
- Confectioners' sugar, 1 pound
- 1 tsp. unsweetened pure vanilla extract
- A pinch of salt
- 1 tbsp. room temperature heavy cream
- Gel food coloring in black, red, and green

For Frankenstein's sake

- 1 cup small chocolate chips, for use in the hair
- Eye-catching chocolate sandwich cookies

- For pupils, brown M&M's or chocolate chips
- Black icing for scars, brows, and lips
- Miniature chocolate sandwich biscuit, suitable for the nose
- Licorice rods for use with bolts

For Frankenstein's Bride

- Hair curls made of white chocolate
- Chocolate sandwich cookies in the shape of eyes and ears
- Darkening the pupils, eyelashes, and scars with black icing
- Miniature chocolate chunks, for use in the hair
- Red icing for the mouth

Directions

Create a cake

1. heat oven 350 degrees F. Butter an 8 1/2-by-4-inch loaf pan. Sprinkle with flour and tap and rotate pan to coat lightly. Excess should be tapped off.
2. Whisk flour, baking powder, and salt in a mixing bowl.
3. Melt 2 tbsp butter in a medium bowl, then whisk in brown sugar and cinnamon.
4. Whisk the remaining 14 tbsp butter and granulated sugar in a large mixing basin with a 3 minute electric mixer until light and frothy. Slowly add eggs, beating well between each addition. Add vanilla extract.
5. Alternate adding flour and milk in three additions, mixing until just mixed.
6. Stir 3/4 cup batter into the bowl with the cinnamon mixture until mixed. Spread half of the leftover batter equally in the prepared loaf

pan. Spread cinnamon batter in an equal layer. Spread the remaining vanilla batter evenly. Swirl a figure-eight pattern in the cake using a little offset spatula or bread knife.

7. Bake for 70–75 minutes, or until a wooden pick inserted in the center comes out clean. Allow for 10 minutes before inverting onto a wire rack to thoroughly cool. Chill the cake at least an hour before icing to minimize crumbs.

Prepare to frost

1. In a large mixing bowl, beat butter until smooth. Beat in cream cheese until smooth (do not overbeat). Beat confectioners' sugar, vanilla, and salt on low speed until well combined. If the mixture is too thick to spread, add cream 1/2 teaspoon at a time. If not immediately used, cover and store in the refrigerator for up to 3 days. Frosting can be softened in the microwave in short bursts at 50% power.

To decorate

1. Arrange cold cake on the serving dish. Coat lightly with 1/2 cup icing, using an offset spatula to smooth the sides and corners. Refrigerate for 20 minutes.
2. In the meantime, color 1/4 cup of icing black in a small bowl. Tint 1/4 cup frosting red in a second bowl (for the bride only). Both frostings should be transferred to piping bags fitted with size 2 or 3 tips. Tint leftover frosting green in the third bowl.
3. Smooth the green icing evenly over the top of the cake (save a little for the nose). While the frosting is still sticky, construct hair with small chocolate chips.

4. For the eyes of Frankenstein, divide biscuits and cut the cream side in half; garnish with chocolate pupils. Pipe scars, brows, and mouth with black icing. Cover the small cookie with the leftover green icing to create a nose. Gently press licorice rods into the cake's side to serve as bolts.

For bride:

1. Add white chocolate curls to the bride's hair. Divide two tiny biscuits in half and expose the cream sides for eyeballs; use some black icing for pupils. Cut one tiny cookie in half and press lightly into the sides of the cake to create ears. Create eyelashes and a scar with black frosting. Make a mouth using crimson icing.

Witch Cupcakes

YIELDS: 2 dozen

TOTAL TIME: 1 hour 0 mins

Ingredients

- Cupcakes chocolate
- Buttercream Vanilla
- Food coloring gel
- Cupcake liners in black
- Mini cupcake liners in black
- Two-sided tape
- Toothpicks

Directions

1. Bake cupcakes as directed and cool thoroughly. Buttercream should be prepared and tinted to desired hues. Cupcakes should be frosted.

2. To create the witches' hats: One cupcake liner should be folded in half and then in half again. Tape together the two flaps to create a solid wedge shape. Again, fold the wedge in half and tape it to form a cone.

3. Insert a toothpick into the frosted cupcake and top with the cone. This is the hat's crown.

4. Punctuate the center of the little cupcake liner. This is the hat's foundation. Slide the cut-out small cupcake liner onto the cone to build the hat. Rep with the remainder of the cupcakes.

Spiderweb Cupcakes

YIELDS: 2 dozen

Ingredients

- Cupcakes chocolate
- Ganache chocolate
- Chocolate white
- M&Ms
- Icing Royale

Directions

1. Bake cupcakes as directed and cool thoroughly.
2. Prepare chocolate ganache and spoon equally over cupcakes; put aside for 30 minutes to set.
3. Parchment paper or a nonstick baking sheet.
4. Microwave white chocolate on 50% power in 30-second intervals until melted and smooth, stirring in between. Transfer to a freezer bag with a

resealable cover and snip off one corner. Pipe spiderwebs onto the prepared sheet, finishing with an M&M spider with royal icing legs and eyes. Allow cooling completely before transferring to individual cupcakes.

Fossil Cookies

YIELDS: 1 dozen

Ingredients

- Simple Sugar Cookies
- Cookies with Black Cocoa
- Approximately 2/3 cup confectioners' sugar
- 2 tablespoons water
- 1 tbsp. sweetened condensed milk
- Colorants for food

Directions

1. Break up the cookie dough as suggested on the packaging. Gently press plastic toy insects into each cookie, chill until firm, then bake according to the manufacturer's instructions and cool completely.
2. Begin by making the glaze. Combine sugar, water, and heavy cream in a mixing bowl until sugar is completely dissolved and no lumps remain. Adjust with additional water as needed and, if desired, tint with food coloring.
3. Arrange cookies on a wire rack set on parchment paper and drizzle with glaze. Push it away from the sides of the cookies with a spoon.

Dark Chocolate Candy Cookies

YIELDS: 5 dozen

TOTAL TIME: 1 hour 0 mins

Ingredients

- 1 1/4 cup unbleached all-purpose flour
- 2/3 cup cocoa powder, Dutch-process
- 1 tsp. baking powder
- kosher salt, 1/4 tsp.
- 1/2 cup room temperature unsalted butter
- 3/4 cup granulated light brown sugar
- 1/4 cup sugar, granulated
- 1 big, room-temperature egg
- 1 tsp. vanilla extract
- 2 ounces bittersweet chocolate, roughly chopped
- 12 small matcha tea KitKats, sliced

Directions

1. Preheat oven to 350°F. Line baking pans with parchment paper. Whisk together flour, cocoa, baking powder, and salt in a medium bowl.
2. In a large mixing bowl, beat butter and sugars with an electric mixer until light and fluffy, about 3 minutes. Reduce mixer speed to low and add the egg and vanilla extract, followed by the flour mixture, mixing until combined. Combine chopped chocolate and KitKats in a separate bowl.
3. Drop dough onto prepared baking sheets, spacing 2 inches apart, and chill for at least 20 minutes until cool.

4. Bake, rotating pans halfway through, for 8 to 10 minutes, or until cookies are puffy and just set. Allow for 2 minutes on the baking sheet before transferring to a wire rack to cool fully.

Pecan Pie Bars

YIELDS:20

TOTAL TIME:1 hour 0 mins

Ingredients

For crust

- 1 cup (2 sticks) room temperature unsalted butter
- 1/2 cup brown sugar, packed
- 1 teaspoon kosher salt
- 2 1/2 cup unbleached all-purpose flour

For purposes of filling

- 1 1/2 cup (1 stick) unsalted butter, cubed
- 1 cup dark brown sugar, packed
- 1 tbsp. honey
- 2 tablespoons bourbon
- 2 tbsp. double cream
- 1 teaspoon kosher salt
- 1 tbsp. unsweetened vanilla extract
- 3 cup coarsely chopped pecan halves

Directions

heat oven 350 degrees F. Coat a 9-by-13-inch baking pan lightly with cooking spray. Line with parchment paper, allowing overhang on two long sides; nonstick spray parchment.

Whisk butter, brown sugar, and salt until light and fluffy with an electric mixer to make the crust. Slowly add flour until little clumps form. Incorporate into the bottom of the prepared pan. Prick holes all over with a fork and bake for 20 to 25 minutes, or until light golden brown. Allow cooling while preparing the filling.

Combine butter, sugar, honey, bourbon, heavy cream, and salt in a small saucepan over low heat to make the filling. Bring to a boil on high heat; continue boiling for 2 minutes. Remove from heat and whisk in vanilla extract, followed by the pecans.

Return to oven and bake until nuts are golden brown and rims are bubbling about 25 to 30 minutes. Allow it cool completely in the pan before transferring it to a cutting board and cutting it into pieces using the overhangs.

Bat Sandwich Cookies

YIELDS: 1 dozen

Ingredients

- Cookies with Black Cocoa
- Icing Royale
- Black sanding sugar, used for decorative purposes
- Buttercream Vanilla

Directions

1. Prepare cookie dough as directed. Cut out bats using cocoa-coated bat cutters. Bake as directed on package and cool thoroughly.

2. Decorate the bottom half of half the cookies with black-tinted royal icing and sprinkle with sanding sugar. Vanilla buttercream is used to fill the sandwich.

Graveyard Cupcakes

YIELDS: 2 dozen

Ingredients

- Cupcakes chocolate
- Buttercream Chocolate
- Chocolate cookies that have been crushed (such as Famous Wafers)
- Cookies purchased in stores (chocolate-covered graham crackers, shortbread cookies, vanilla-and-chocolate sandwich cookies) (such as Milanos)
- Royal Icing for decorative purposes

Directions

1. Bake cupcakes according to package directions and cool completely. Frost with chocolate buttercream gently pushes crushed chocolate cookie "dirt" into the frosting.

2. Using white royal icing on chocolate cookies and black royal icing on vanilla cookies, pipe dates, or RIP on each cookie to resemble gravestones, then press into dirt-covered cupcakes.

Black and Red Crinkle Cookies

YIELDS: 3 dozen

TOTAL TIME: 1 hour 0 mins

Ingredients

- 1 1/2 cup unbleached all-purpose flour
- 2 tablespoons unsweetened cocoa powder, with additional for coating
- 1 tsp. baking powder
- 1 teaspoon kosher salt
- Cinnamon, 1/2 tsp.
- 1 and a quarter cup granulated sugar
- 4 tbsp. (1/2 stick) melted unsalted butter
- 1/2 teaspoon gelled red food coloring
- 1 tsp. essence vanilla
- two big eggs

Directions

1. Sift together flour, cocoa powder, baking powder, salt, and cinnamon in a medium bowl.
2. Whisk together granulated sugar, butter, food coloring, vanilla extract, and eggs in a large mixing dish. Fold in the flour mixture with a spatula. Wrap bowl in plastic wrap and chill for about 30 minutes (it will still be soft).
3. Preheat oven to 375 °F. 2 parchment-lined baking sheets

4. In a shallow bowl, place some cocoa powder. Roll tsp of dough into balls and dip completely with cocoa before transferring to prepared baking sheets, spacing 3 inches apart.
5. Bake 12 to 14 minutes, or until cookies are slightly stiff to the touch. Allow 10 minutes for cooling on the baking pan. Rep with the remainder of the dough.

Mummy Cupcakes

YIELDS: 2 dozen

Ingredients

- Cupcakes chocolate
- Buttercream Vanilla
- Gel food coloring in green and black
- Eyeballs made with candy

Directions

1. Bake cupcakes according to package directions and cool completely.
2. Prepare buttercream and dye it with green and black food coloring. Transfer the bowl contents to a piping bag fitted with a ribbon tip.
3. Pipe buttercream back and forth across each cupcake, resembling a mummy's wrapping. Each should have two sweet eyeballs.

Chocolate and Pumpkin Ice Cream Sandwiches

YIELDS: 8 servings

TOTAL TIME: 2 hours 30 mins

Ingredients

- Pumpkin ice cream or gelato, 2 pt.
- 4 graham crackers, chocolate, quartered to make rectangles
- 4 ounces chopped bittersweet chocolate

Directions

1. Allow 10 min for the ice cream to get to room temperature. Wrap the loaf pan in plastic wrap and freeze for at least 2 hours until solid.
2. Remove ice cream from pan and wrap in plastic wrap. Sandwich two graham crackers together. Freeze until ready to serve.
3. Microwave chocolate on 50% power in 30-second intervals until melted and smooth, stirring in between. Drizzle the dressing over the sandwiches just before serving.

Chocolate Skeleton Cookies

YIELDS: 3 dozen
TOTAL TIME: 0 hours 55 mins

Ingredients

- 1 and a half cups all-purpose flour
- 1/4 cup cocoa, unsweetened
- 1/2 cup unsweetened black cocoa
- 1/2 tsp. bicarbonate of soda
- 1 tablespoon kosher salt
- Approximately 3/4 cup unsalted butter

- 3/4 cup sugar, granulated
- a single huge egg
- Pure vanilla extract, 2 tsp.
- Royal Icing, for use in decorating

Directions

1. Whisk flour, cocoa powder, baking soda, and salt in a medium bowl.

2. In a large mixing bowl, cream butter and sugar with an electric mixer until fluffy, about 3 minutes. Incorporate the egg, followed by the vanilla. Reduce speed to low and add flour mixture in a slow, steady stream, mixing until completely combined.

3. Divide dough into two disks and roll each one to a thickness of 1/8 inch between two pieces of waxed paper. Chill 30 minutes in the refrigerator or 15 minutes in the freezer until hard.

4. Preheat oven to 350 degrees F. Preheat oven to 350°F. Line baking pans with parchment paper. Cut out cookies using cocoa-dusted cookie cutters. Arrange on prepared baking sheets. Reroll, freeze, and trim scraps as necessary.

5. Bake, rotating baking sheets halfway through, for 10 to 12 minutes, or until cookies are lightly golden brown around the edges. Allow 5 minutes for cooling on sheets before transferring to wire racks to cool completely.

6. Prepare royal frosting as directed on the package. Pipe bones with a piping bag with a small round tip. Allow drying.

Stuffed Dark Chocolate Whoopie Pies

YIELDS: 14 servings

TOTAL TIME: 0 hours 50 mins

Ingredients

- 1 cup unbleached all-purpose flour
- 1/4 cup cocoa powder, unsweetened
- 3/4 tsp. bicarbonate of soda
- 1/4 tsp. bicarbonate of soda
- 1/4 tablespoon kosher salt
- 1/2 cup light brown sugar, packed
- 4 tbsp unsalted butter, room temp
- a single huge egg
- 1 and a half cups milk
- 2 tablespoons buttercream frosting
- 1 and 1/2 c. Mini M&M's

Directions

1. Preheat oven to 375 °F. Preheat oven to 350°F. Line baking pans with parchment paper. Combine flour, cocoa powder, baking soda, and salt in a medium basin.
2. In a large mixing bowl, whisk brown sugar and butter with an electric mixer until light and fluffy, about 3 minutes. Incorporate egg. Alternately add the flour mixture and milk, mixing well.
3. Drop batter by level tablespoons onto prepared baking sheets, spreading them 2 inches apart. Bake 6 to 8 min, or until the tops are firm, and spring back when lightly touched. Allow 5 minutes for cooling on baking sheets before transferring to a wire rack to cool entirely.

4. Pipe a thick rope of frosting around the outside rims of the flat sides of six whoopie pie halves using a pastry bag or resealable bag. Refrigerate for approximately 15 minutes or until firm. Each half should have 1 tbsp M&M's Minis in the center, followed by the remaining halves.

Chocolate Pumpkin Cake

CAL/SERV:630

YIELDS:12

PREP TIME:0 hours 35 mins

TOTAL TIME:1 hour 30 mins

Ingredients

- 1 and a half cups all-purpose flour
- 3/4 cup cocoa, unsweetened
- 1 1/2 tsp. bicarbonate of soda
- 1/4 teaspoon salt
- 1 cup fat-free buttermilk
- 3/4 cup pure canned pumpkin
- 2 c. sugar, granular
- Three big eggs
- Brown Butter Glaze

Directions

Prepare the cake as follows: Preheat the oven to 350 degrees Fahrenheit. Grease two 8-inch round cake pans. Preheat oven to 350°F. Line bottoms with parchment paper and oil. Flour the pans.

Combine flour, cocoa, baking soda, and salt in a large mixing basin. Whisk together buttermilk, pumpkin, and vanilla extract in a medium mixing basin. In a large mixing basin, whip butter and sugar on low speed until combined. Increase to high speed and beat for 5 minutes or until pale and fluffy, scraping the bowl regularly with a rubber spatula. Reduce to a medium-low speed and add eggs one at a time, beating thoroughly after each addition. Add flour mixture first, then buttermilk mixture, finishing with flour mixture beat on low speed just until batter is smooth, scraping bowl occasionally with a rubber spatula.

Distribute batter evenly between prepared baking pans. Bake 30–35 min, or until a toothpick inserted in the center comes out clean. Allow 10 minutes for cooling in pans on wire racks. Loosen layers from sides of pans with a tiny knife; invert onto wire racks. Remove and discard paper carefully; allow to cool completely, about 45 minutes. Wrapped in plastic, layers can be stored at room temperature for up to 1 day or in the freezer for 1 month. Before decorating, bring to room temperature.

Meanwhile, create Brown Butter Frosting; tint to desired shade using orange gel food coloring. On a cake stand, place 1 cake layer. Spread one-third of the icing evenly on top. Top with a second cake layer. Distribute leftover frosting evenly across the top and sides of the cake. The cake can be kept covered in the fridge for 3 days.

Printed in Great Britain
by Amazon